Guide Dogs for the Blind

Looking Ahead

Text by Paula Harrington

Guide Dogs for the Blind, San Rafael, California

First Edition

For information contact:
Guide Dogs for the Blind, Inc.
350 Los Ranchitos Road
P.O. Box 151200
San Rafael, Calif. 94915-1200

Library of Congress Catalog Card Number:
90-81022

ISBN: 0-9626144-0-8

First Edition

**Guide Dogs for the Blind warmly invites you
to visit the San Rafael campus. Information
on graduation day ceremonies and on arrang-
ing campus and kennel tours is available by
telephoning (415) 499-4000.**

Production Coordinated by
Mrs. Malcolm T. Dungan
Edited by Jan Ford
Designed by John Giannotti
Typeset by Frank's Type, Inc.
Printed by Sandler/Becker, Inc.

This book was typeset in ITC Berkeley Old Style Book.

Dedicated to the friends of Guide Dogs for the Blind

Acknowledgments

This book would not have been possible without the help of many staff members and students of Guide Dogs for the Blind, Inc., who made themselves available for long interviews during my research, interrupting their professional and personal lives. Their time is greatly appreciated.

The Historical Committee of the Board of Directors of Guide Dogs for the Blind initiated this history and oversaw the project from conception to completion. Committee chairman Nancy Dungan and members Joanne Blokker, Ann Cuneo, Olga Dollar, Diana Rossi and Walt Stewart attended long meetings and offered excellent editorial suggestions. Each contributed in many places to the text.

A special debt of gratitude is owed Thom Ainsworth, chief operations officer. He spent many hours tracking down old records, files and photographs on his own and at my request. His help has been invaluable in making this history as complete, accurate and true to the spirit of Guide Dogs as possible. — P.H.

The Historical Committee of Guide Dogs for the Blind on the Guide Dogs campus. Seated are, left, chairman Nancy Dungan and Olga Dollar. Standing are, left, Joanne Blokker, Ann Cuneo, Diana Rossi and chief operations officer Thom Ainsworth. At Mrs. Dungan's right is "Kai," a black Labrador retriever breeder. At her feet is "Samantha," a golden retriever career-change dog. Between Mrs. Dungan and Mrs. Dollar is "Bev," a career-change German shepherd; and on Mrs. Dollar's left is "Flapper," a yellow Lab breeder. Not pictured are committee members Genelle Relfe and Walt Stewart.
—Photo by Michael Scannell

Contents

Kate Del Ross and yellow Labrador retriever Guide Dog "Folger" descend the steps of an airliner on the way to take the rigorous state examination that qualified Ms. Del Ross as a licensed instructor. "Folger" is pictured with his puppy raiser, Katherine Gordon of Rancho Palos Verdes, Calif., on p. 60.

Preface: *Presenting the New Teams: Graduation Day, 1990, San Rafael, California*

"What is it about Guide Dogs for the Blind that creates an atmosphere in which that kind of love can be exchanged? When we come here, we can only gain independence by letting go of our fear and learning to trust our dogs."
— *Guide Dog Student Justin Mc Devitt*

At first, it looks like an outdoor graduation ceremony at any small college. Then, you start to notice the dogs.

Golden retrievers, Labrador retrievers and German shepherds, the three breeds trained as Guide Dogs, are among the audience gathered on the lawn. Their carefully brushed coats shimmer in the California sun. The dogs wearing the green 4-H jackets identifying them as Guide Dog puppies range in age from three months to a year or more. Adult breeding stock dogs and career-change dogs are there with their human families. On stage, facing the audience, a row of dogs will sit in harness next to the graduates and the 4-H Club members who raised the dogs will stand behind the graduates. The scene will shortly become an unforgettable tableau. After graduation, both dog and blind person will go home and start their lives together.

These dogs are not only an accepted part of the graduation day ritual; they are the very reason it exists. Since Guide Dogs for the Blind, Inc., was founded in 1942, the staff has trained more than 6,000 dogs to help blind people gain increased mobility.

Blind people using dogs as guides is not new. The first image of a dog used as a guide was found in Pompeii in a painting on the wall of a house buried by volcanic lava in 79 A.D. The image has recurred in the art of different ages and cultures, for example, in a 13th-century Chinese scroll, a medieval painting, Rembrandt drawings and a 19th-century French lithograph.

Before World War II, few, if any, formal mobility programs existed. The Seeing Eye of Morristown, New Jersey, founded in 1929, was the first recognized dog guide school in the United States.

Since it was founded in 1942 with one trainer, two students and donated dogs, Guide Dogs for the Blind has continually refined its program and expanded its facilities. Guide Dogs has a staff of 103, a kennel for 300 purebred dogs and puppies and a dormitory for 24 students. Twelve classes, each lasting four weeks, are held every year. Each class, typically, has 16 first-time students and 8 students returning to receive new dogs to replace those who are no longer able to act as guides.

Everywhere on the Guide Dogs' campus, sight is superseded by other senses. The gardens are filled with fragrant plants. Water gurgles in an artificial pond. Walkways in the center of the campus are paved in aggregate, which feels different underfoot than the smooth cement sidewalks that lead off campus.

At a recent graduation ceremony, valedictorian Justin McDevitt, a management training specialist from Minnesota, described how much the school means to those it serves. Led to the microphone by his first Guide Dog, a golden retriever named "Dugan," he began with stories of how nervous and clumsy they had all been in the first days of class, then his light-hearted tone yielded to seriousness.

At the conclusion of the ceremony, the 4-H members who raised the dogs stand behind the graduates and their new Guide Dogs. From left are graduate David Collins of Encinitas, Calif., with "Paris," graduate Charlotte Diggs of Austin, Texas, with "Cruiser," and graduate Daniel Emlaw of San Diego, Calif. with "Elder." In the back row, raiser Jeanne Cannon of Ramona, Calif., also a 4-H project leader, wipes away a tear and raiser Katherine Gordon of Rancho Palos Verdes, Calif., beams her pride at the audience.
—Photo by Jim Gordon

"I see love being given and received in a real and active sense here. It is a love that meets a need and I think that is the greatest love of all," he said.

"What is it about Guide Dogs for the Blind that creates an atmosphere in which that kind of love can be exchanged? When we come here, we can only gain independence by letting go of our fear and learning to trust our dogs."

As the valedictorian spoke, it became clear why the audience, sighted and blind, looked so touched by his words. The blind people who come to Guide Dogs face issues that concern everyone: how much to depend on others, how to live autonomously.

The goal of Guide Dogs for the Blind—"mobility based on trust"—sounds straightforward enough. But it requires what must be the most difficult state to attain in life for people of all backgrounds and abilities: the willingness to change and grow.

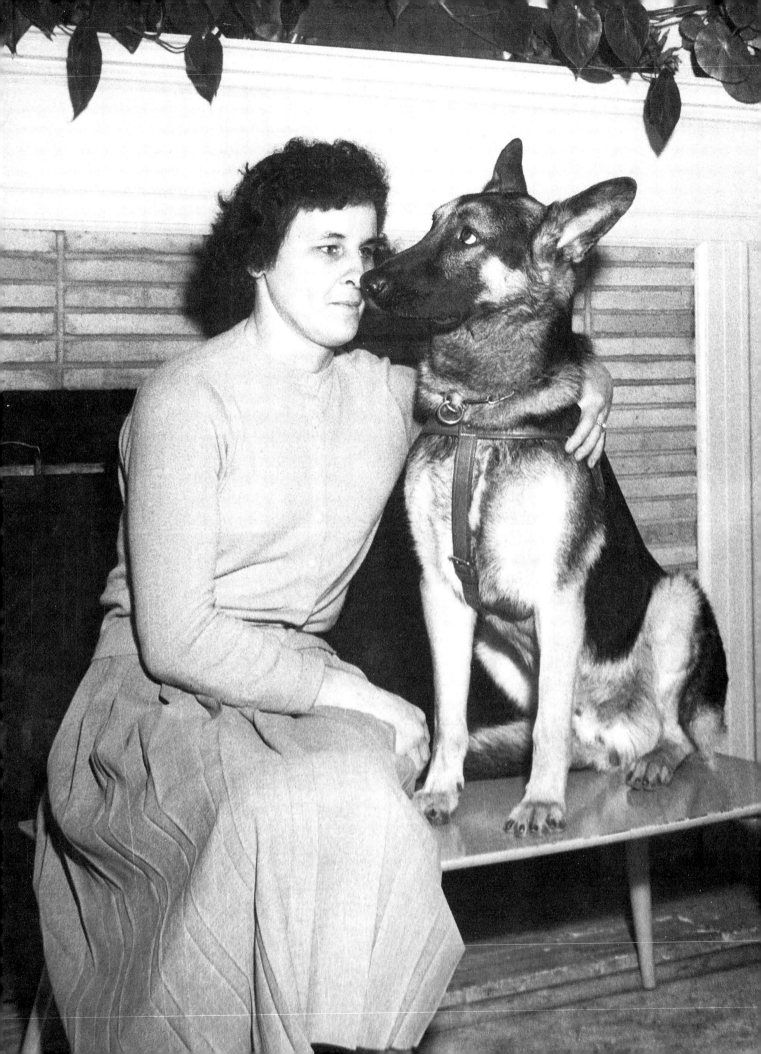

I. Early Days (1941–1946)

"I am a darkroom technician at Stanford Medical Center in Palo Alto, California, where I have lived for 20 years. I have been blind almost since birth.

I first came to Guide Dogs for the Blind in the summer of 1943, when I was 18. The school was then located in an old rented house in Los Gatos. I was in the second class and I remember there were just three students. Don Donaldson was the only instructor; Lois Merrihew was his assistant.

Looking back, if you asked me why I wanted to get a dog, instead of using a cane as most blind people did in those days, I would have to say it was because of my mother. She always had to have a dog in our house. And she raised me to believe I could go out and do pretty much what I wanted. So when I heard about dogs being used as guides, it seemed like a natural thing for me to do.

Right from the beginning, I had confidence in the school. But in those early days it was harder to be accepted in public with a Guide Dog. People wouldn't let us in restaurants, for example. Other people were so curious, they'd come up to us on the street and ask us all sorts of questions.

I remember once I went into a store in Los Gatos with two other students— that was our task for the day. We'd decided to go to the lunch counter and have milkshakes. Our dogs led us in and waited patiently at our feet, just as they were supposed to. But their presence caused quite a stir.

The school was so small then it was natural for those involved with it to feel a special bond. We understood that we were engaged together in an exciting new endeavor. People thought we were a little odd maybe, but we didn't pay much attention. We thought of ourselves as trailblazers.

I'll never forget that Lois Merrihew —who was only about my age—used to read to us every night. Today, the school has a reading room well stocked with Braille editions of magazines and books, but we didn't have any of that yet. There weren't as many cars in those days, either; Los Gatos was pretty rural. So some of the obstacles we had to deal with were different. For example, there was less traffic and noise and fewer structures. But there also weren't as many sidewalks or curbs to help us find our way.

After I got my first dog, a German shepherd named 'Polly,' my life had fewer limitations. That has been true ever since. I went on to work for the Navy at the Alameda Naval Air Station as the Navy's first blind aircraft mechanic. I later left the service to get married and raise two children. The dogs made a tremendous difference in my ability to do all that.

Over the years, I have come back to Guide Dogs each time I needed a new guide. I've just received my sixth dog. I remember every one of them. There was 'Polly,' followed by three more German shepherds; 'Johnny,' 'Kerry' and 'Bumper.' Then I had a yellow Labrador retriever named 'Jacob.' Now I have a shepherd named 'Mozart.'

Betty Mantooth and "Johnny" in 1957. He was her second Guide Dog.
—Photo Courtesy of Betty Mantooth

"The school was so small then it was natural for those involved with it to feel a special bond. We understood that we were engaged together in an exciting new endeavor. People thought we were a little odd maybe, but we didn't pay much attention. We thought of ourselves as trailblazers."
—Betty Mantooth

Each dog is different. For instance, they've all had a different walk. I can think back to each one and how it felt in harness — what its gait was like, the feel of being led by that particular dog. They're all individuals.

Some schools and other institutions don't necessarily get better as they get bigger. Guide Dogs definitely has. The kennels have improved. The training has improved. Everything has improved over the years. That's the way it should be, I think.

For me, a woman in her sixties who has used Guide Dogs for more than 40 years, the school is a permanent part of my life. It's a place I return to from time to time, like you might to college reunions or the town where you grew up. It's been a second home. And every time I've returned has been a learning experience. Because even when you've used Guide Dogs as long as I have, you can't assume you know all the answers. You have to start with a blank slate if you want to create a true bond with your new dog. The way I look at it is this: You find a good school; you keep going there."

— Betty Mantooth

Betty Mantooth with "Mozart" in 1988. "Mozart" is her sixth Guide Dog; all but "Jacob," a yellow Labrador retriever, have been German shepherd dogs.
—Photo by Thom Ainsworth

1. A West Coast Guide Dog School

Many newly blinded members of the military were sent home after the intense fighting in the Pacific Theater during World War II. The founders of Guide Dogs for the Blind anticipated that these veterans could benefit from a West Coast school.

While The Seeing Eye dog guide school had been in operation for some time in Morristown, New Jersey, no such school had been established in the West and blind veterans faced an additional trip across the country to obtain a dog guide. The situation prompted two groups to join forces — those skilled in dog training and those devoted to charitable work.

In 1941, a dog guide trainer named Chalmers R. Donaldson and called "Don" had taken as a student a young Pasadena woman, Lois Merrihew. Mr. Donaldson was one of only 10 dog guide trainers in the country.

For Miss Merrihew, this was the re-alization of her childhood goal. She had been fascinated by the idea of training dogs to lead the blind ever since reading a book on the subject as a young girl. After she graduated from junior college, she attended a lecture by dog trainer Hazel Hurst.

"I walked right up to her afterwards and asked if she wanted to start a school," Miss Merrihew recalled.

The school, the now-defunct Hazel Hurst Foundation, opened in 1939 in Monrovia, a suburb of Los Angeles, with Miss Merrihew serving as lecturer, fund-raiser and even driver of its station wagon. She then persuaded Don Donaldson to train her as a dog guide instructor. The arduous training lasted four years, during which she spent a full month under blind-fold. Her guide was "Blondie," a female German shepherd she had rescued from the Pasadena Humane Society.

She left the Hazel Hurst Foundation in the summer of 1941 to train with Mr. Donaldson in Northern California. There, they began to pursue a new goal: to found their own dog guide school near San Francisco.

While they sought financial backing to pursue that goal, Miss Merrihew worked behind the cigarette counter at the Fairmont Hotel atop Nob Hill in San Francisco and Mr. Donaldson worked in a shipyard in Palo Alto.

She found a patron in D.M. Linnard, the hotel's owner. He agreed to lend an office in the Fairmont to her and Mr. Don-aldson and provided the services of the hotel's publicity director, A.S. Oko, Jr. With Mr. Oko's help, they soon accom-plished a minor publicity miracle with a single photograph that was taken at the nearby Sir Francis Drake Hotel and pub-lished in the *San Francisco Chronicle* on Oct. 21, 1941. The accompanying story announced that Mr. Donaldson was seek-ing contributions for a school to be founded in the San Francisco area.

Pearl Harbor was bombed on Dec. 7, 1941, less than two months later. On that day, Miss Merrihew, Mr. Donaldson and Mr. Oko were riding down California Street, not far from the Fairmont.

"We heard the bulletin on the radio about Pearl Harbor and the U.S. entering the war," she said. "Mr. Oko immediately turned to me and said that the men blinded in the attack would be coming back to San Francisco."

The next day, Miss Merrihew and Mr. Donaldson visited Letterman Army Medical Center to offer their services to a wartime organization known as American Women's Voluntary Services. The A.W.V.S. volunteer spirit soon combined with the expertise of Miss Merrihew and Mr. Donaldson to form the foundation of the Guide Dogs program. As Mr. Oko had

Clipping from San Francisco Chronicle, Oct. 21, 1941.

A Dog Leads the Way

When she descended the Sir Francis Drake Hotel's marble stairway yesterday pretty blindfolded Miss Lois Merrihew had no fear. Guiding her to safety through crowds of onlookers was a German shepherd, trained to emancipate the sightless. Miss Merrihew is the only woman serving an apprenticeship in guide dog training for the blind. Her tutor is C. R. Donaldson, who is seeking to establish a local training school for guide dogs and the blind.

Aid for Blind: Girl Will Train Dogs to Act as Guides

A very pretty girl descended the marble steps of the Sir Francis Drake Hotel yesterday.

Ordinarily such descents cause little or no stir of excitement. San Francisco has many pretty girls; many flights of marble steps.

But the scene yesterday was different.

The girl was blindfolded. And leading her was a German shepherd dog.

The little interlude was one of the highlights of the luncheon meeting of the Associated Business Girls of California at which Miss Lois Merrihew was one of the speakers.

Miss Merrihew is the first woman in the United States to serve an apprenticeship in guide dog training for the blind.

She was introduced at the luncheon by her tutor, C. R. Donaldson, who has undertaken to train approximately 30 per cent of the German shepherd dogs now being used by California blind.

At the luncheon meeting Donaldson said that of the 12,000 blind in California there are probably 2500 who are temperamentally and physically able to use guide dogs.

Donaldson is seeking an adequate site in this area for the immediate establishment of such a training school and assisting him are D. M. Linnard, local hotelman; Mary Cook Cowerd, founder of the National Association for the Advancement of Blind Artists, and H. Sewall Bradley, president of that organization.

joined the Marines, Constance Edwards of San Francisco took over generating publicity for the group. She was also instrumental in the passage of state licensing legislation under which Guide Dogs for the Blind, Inc. became the first such school licensed in California.

By the spring of 1942, enough money had been raised to open the fledgling school. It was incorporated on May 27, 1942, and the first board of directors was appointed. Mr. Donaldson was named instructor and Miss Merrihew was named his assistant. Guide Dogs for the Blind was ready to open its doors.

The A.W.V.S., directed by Mrs. Ryer Nixon, national representative; and Mrs. Nion Tucker, San Francisco chairperson, third and fourth from the left, was interested in establishing a dog guide school for the blinded veterans. The team of Donaldson and Merrihew conducted A.W.V.S. training classes, lectured and sponsored benefit events for interested donors in the planned school.
—Photo from Guide Dogs for the Blind Archives

2. *Tilted Acres*

The school's first home was a rented two-story Victorian house in Los Gatos, southwest of San Jose. The town was still rural and the house, the caretaker's cottage and 12 acres of rolling hills had once been the Owen Atkinson estate and was called Tilted Acres. A small horse stable was converted into a kennel.

The school began with four German shepherds, "Blondie;" "Fraula," donated by her Santa Rosa owner; "Penny," the gift of a San Rafael resident; and "Connie," who came from the San Francisco dog pound.

The first few years were frugal while fundraising activities continued. During the first year, $8,672.79 was raised.

Nine students received training at Tilted Acres and several dogs were trained for additional use.

Top
Guide Dogs moved to its second Los Gatos location after two years at Tilted Acres. Lois Merrihew and Don Donaldson each had a class of four students.
—Photo from Guide Dogs for the Blind Archives

Bottom
This is Guide Dogs' first home, an old Victorian farm house called "Tilted Acres." The school began there with four donated German shepherds.
—Photo from Guide Dogs for the Blind Archives

The second class, which entered that July and graduated in August, contained three students. Betty June Taylor, now Betty Mantooth, worked at the Alameda Naval Air Station sewing aircraft wing coverings. Alan Jenkins had graduated from a local junior college and planned to attend the University of California, Berkeley. Earling Loftquist was a shift foreman who had worked on the Hetch Hetchy Dam before he lost his sight.

Named as officers of the new organization were Mrs. Ryer Nixon as president; Mrs. John Breeden, Mrs. Frank Deering, Mrs. Nion Tucker and the Honorable Florence Kahn.

The third class, held in September and October, included World War II veteran Sgt. Leonard Foulk, age 26, who had lost his sight at the battle of Attu. He graduated with "Blondie," the dog Miss Merrihew had originally rescued from the Pasadena pound and who had served as her guide in early fundraising and publicity demonstrations.

Guide Dogs for the Blind's first class consisted of two students, Lemoyne Cox of Oakland and Marjorie Cosgrove of San Francisco. The class graduated on June 1, 1942. Don Donaldson stands at the top of the stairs. Mr. Cox was a typewriter repairman and mechanic at a local defense plant. His dog was "Lady." Mrs. Cosgrove was the wife of a Navy man in combat overseas, and her dog, "Vicki," served as her guide for the next eight years.
—Photo from Guide Dogs for the Blind Archives

Guide Dogs soon received its first donation from a grateful graduate, Marjorie Cosgrove, who wrote, "I only wish that somebody else may some day be as happy as I am with a dog." Meanwhile, formal fundraising was established as a way to build operating revenues. For example, a card party at the Fairmont Hotel brought in $2,448.25.

Guide Dogs not only needed ways to raise money, it needed to obtain enough dogs for training. Pleas went out in 1944 for donated dogs appropriate for the program and for people to help raise puppies. The response was immediate and gratifying: 79 people had volunteered to raise puppies by 1945.

During Guide Dogs' first two years, 27 dogs had been given to graduates, including three veterans, several college students and working people, among them a field worker for the blind and a musician.

Sgt. Leonard Foulk, the first veteran to receive a Guide Dog, was blinded when he raised his head from his foxhole during the battle of Attu and a Japanese sniper shot the binoculars he was holding, destroying his optic nerve. His dog was "Blondie." He was awarded the Bronze Star for extreme bravery in action for saving the lives of his mortar division during that battle.
—Photo from Guide Dogs for the Blind Archives

3. The Second Los Gatos Location

After two years at the rented Tilted Acres, Guide Dogs bought its first property, an old house on Foster Road in Los Gatos. The house, which cost $12,000, had eight rooms, two baths and 26 acres of cultivated grounds. The monthly payments on the property, after a down payment, were the same as the rent paid for Tilted Acres.

The house was renovated for the convenience of students and dogs. At the same time, a series of staff changes was under way. Mr. Donaldson retired and Miss Merrihew, then 24 years old, was named director. Stewart Wiest, another experienced dog trainer, replaced her as instructor. Mr. Wiest had been stationed with the Army K-9 Corps in San Carlos during World War II.

Before joining Guide Dogs, Mr. Wiest had been "training dogs for a number of service men without sight, because the Army figured it would do the training itself," he recalled. "But the program eventually fell through."

Clarence Pfaffenberger's breeding program resolved the dog shortage problem, tracked and reproduced genetically the best traits for Guide Dogs and built excellent lines of dogs. Several different breeds were tried out during the first few years. Eventually, the three in use today were decided upon: the golden retriever, the German shepherd and the Labrador retriever, both yellow and black.
—Photo from Guide Dogs for the Blind Archives

When he and his wife, Evelyn, moved to Los Gatos, "it was pretty much the three of us as far as staff was concerned. My wife took care of the house, did the cooking and generally ran the household. She became sort of the housemother, reading mail to the blind students and writing letters for them. The only other staff person was Loutricia Farwell, who was in charge of general management.

"As for the training, Lois and I each had a class of four students. We obtained dogs wherever we could. There was such a shortage then of German shepherds due to their use in the K-9 Corps that we ran ads in local papers for donated dogs. Sometimes, people would simply call and say they had a good dog. Then Lois and I would go out and take a look to see if the dog was healthy and had the right temperament and size."

Clarence J. Pfaffenberger and Eloise Heller, two other dog lovers who were to have a profound impact on the school's future, became involved with Guide Dogs during this time.

A former journalism teacher in San Francisco high schools, Mr. Pfaffenberger had retired to devote himself to the study and the breeding of dogs. He became involved with Guide Dogs through his acquaintance with Eloise Heller, who was assuming a major role within the organization.

Mrs. Heller was working on his volunteer staff at the K-9 Corps and asked him if he could supply dogs to be trained for the blind. He was already supplying dogs to The Seeing Eye in New Jersey and got the Army's permission to supply dogs for Guide Dogs.

Mr. Pfaffenberger originated three crucial parts of the Guide Dogs program during his 21 years as a full-time volunteer—"puppy testing," the use of 4-H Club families to raise the puppies and the Guide Dogs breeding program. He is considered an international authority on dog training, and his puppy testing program is used by all groups working with dogs, including search and rescue groups.

Mr. Pfaffenberger found an able associate in Mrs. Heller, who was already well-known in San Francisco social and philanthropic circles. She began by donating her time out of a love of dogs and an awareness of the program's importance and potential.

She served as president of the Board of Directors from 1947 to 1949 and worked with Mr. Pfaffenberger to establish standards for Guide Dog breeds.

Mrs. Eloise Heller at the San Rafael campus with a Chesapeake Bay retriever, a breed no longer used as a Guide Dog.
—Photo by Les Walsh

4. State Licensing

Lois Merrihew, shown at the wheel of the Guide Dogs for the Blind station wagon in the late 1940s, was the second person in California to be licensed as an instructor. The first was Stewart Wiest.
—Photos from Guide Dogs for the Blind Archives

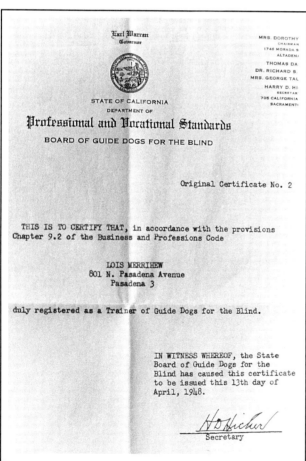

There were no regulations governing either the training of dog guides or teaching of the blind to use them. Blind people in Southern California had registered complaints about inexperienced trainers.

In 1945, Guide Dogs directed its efforts to the establishment of universal standards in the dog guide field. Lois Merrihew, Stewart Wiest and Constance Edwards joined forces to campaign for state legislation that became the first of its kind in the country.

An initial bill, introduced in the California State Assembly in January, 1945, by Albert I. Stewart, did not include regulations for licensing schools and did not gain the support of those in the dog guide field.

"My original feeling was that the legislators in Sacramento did not believe that dogs were as useful to the blind as we already knew they were," Stewart Wiest recalled. "To prove our point, we took a dog with us on one trip to Sacramento and asked an assemblyman, who was sighted, to participate in a demonstration. First we gave him a cane to use. Then we gave him a dog. After a few minutes, everyone could see the difference. That demonstration made all the difference."

On June 8, 1945, the Assembly voted to create a Special Interim Investigating Committee to study and analyze all facets of dog guide training, including the operation of schools.

The final law — House Resolution 2391 — was adopted on Feb. 5, 1947. It established a State Board of Guide Dogs for the Blind, charged with enforcing the high standards outlined by the Interim Investigating Committee for the licensing of trainers and schools in California. Not long after the law took effect, Stewart Wiest received State License #1 and Lois Merrihew received License #2.

5. *The Early Program*

From Guide Dogs' beginnings at Tilted Acres, the organization recognized dog training as a highly specialized skill with consistency as its key. To serve well as guides, dogs must learn to exercise the canine equivalent of judgment.

Through gradual, consistent exposure, Mr. Donaldson, Miss Merrihew and Mr. Wiest taught each dog to identify and avoid obstacles, as the school's trainers do today. As a newspaper account noted, "Every step of guide dog training is based on the constant thought of the future when the dog must follow the commands of a blind master."

The original program was shorter for the dogs, three months instead of five, and the same one-month period for the students. The concept remains the same today: to train the dog in the commands and skills it will need with its licensed trainer, then transfer its loyalty to its new, blind owner during the final month. During that month, the blind student learns to trust the judgment of the dog who is to be his or her guide.

The process can seem slow and frustrating to those first undertaking it; many blind persons have been discouraged during the first days of class. But the discouragement passes as the dog and blind master become a team, a working unit.

The reliability of the program developed at Guide Dogs for the Blind has become a source of assurance for its students. It also pays tribute to those, especially Don Donaldson, Lois Merrihew and Stewart Wiest, who first established it.

A German shepherd Guide Dog helps to break ground for the new San Rafael headquarters of Guide Dogs for the Blind. Kneeling are, from left, Mrs. Nion Tucker, Mrs. Adrian Falk and Francis V. Keesling, Jr. The new campus was made possible by an overwhelmingly successful fundraising campaign in 1946.
—**Photo from Guide Dogs for the Blind Archives**

II. A Permanent Home

"During World War II, I was stationed as a volunteer at the Chelsea Naval Station Hospital outside Boston the night the Marines started coming in from Iwo Jima. I sat for a long time with one young man who had lost his sight. When I got up to leave, he asked me 'Will you come back tomorrow?' I was so touched by his request that I went to the commander and demanded to be trained to provide real help—not just sympathy—to blind veterans.

We soon developed a program for nurses and women volunteers to assist blind Navy men in practical ways. Its purpose was to reach out to the young man lying with his face to the wall so he could tell us what he needed. For example, we might work with him and his young wife on accepting and adjusting to his disability.

How did I get from there to Guide Dogs? After the war, I moved with my husband, retired Major General Pierpont Morgan Hamilton, to California and became involved with volunteer work with the Humane Society. One day, I received a phone call from a friend who was on the Board of Directors of Guide Dogs. He described its program, and, because of my volunteer work with the blind and with animals, I agreed to become the Santa Barbara representative. It turned out to be one of the most important decisions of my life. Before I knew it, I had taken charge of organizing a local fundraiser and was traveling to San Rafael every month. At that time, there were 12 dogs in the kennels and we were still using some donated dogs. The campus held only the old main building, which housed the kitchen, and a dormitory of four beds, plus dog runs and a kennel.

On my first trip to the school, I met Executive Director Bill Johns. Like many of those involved with the founding of Guide Dogs, he had a background in the K-9 Corps. He also had worked at The Seeing Eye in New Jersey. Beyond that, he was what I called the wizard of dogs. He seemed half-canine himself. Because of this skill, he had entree with dog show people and was able to interest them in the work being done at Guide Dogs.

Not long after I began volunteering, however, I came to the conclusion that the school also had to actively promote itself to be successful. So I said to Bill Johns, 'You need a salesman and I'm a good salesman. But, if I'm going to sell, I've got to understand the product.' He asked me what I wanted to know, and I replied, 'For starters, I'd like someone to show me how to clean the kennels.'

He looked at me—in my mink coat and jewelry—and never batted an eye. The next day, he took me over to the kennels and did exactly what I'd asked.

Bill Johns could persuade people like me to devote their energies to Guide Dogs because he was blessed with a talent more valuable to the school than any other. He was a superb showman. He could do simple obedience commands on a stage with a dog that made you believe you were seeing 'Lassie' and 'Rin Tin Tin' combined.

He had initiated a tour program for school representatives to travel to different cities and give presentations before service clubs and organizations. My interest in 'selling' the school led me to that program.

At first, we limited our trips to the Western United States. We usually went for only one week at a time, although I recall one six-week trip to Texas. We also

"Not long after I began volunteering, however, I came to the conclusion that the school also had to actively promote itself to be successful. So I said to Bill Johns, 'You need a salesman and I'm a good salesman. But, if I'm going to sell, I've got to understand the product.' He asked me what I wanted to know, and I replied, 'For starters, I'd like someone to show me how to clean the kennels.'"
—Norah Hamilton Straus

rotated trips, especially later when the school had begun to grow. I would do a tour with Bill Johns, and then one with (current Chief Executive Officer) Bruce Benzler. Had it not been for those tours, I don't think the school would ever have gotten where it did. This regular schedule of tours continued for a period of six or seven years.

We faced a tough task initially, because few people had seen Guide Dogs on the street or understood what the school was doing. Many audiences were polite and helpful, but just as often we were treated as a curiosity or an afterthought to the luncheon announcements. Frequently, my presentation would be left until last and short-changed for time. So I learned quickly not to ask for donations but to take the approach of an educator. After all, we had to tell people about Guide Dogs before we could ask them for money.

The newness of our endeavor led to some humorous moments. I remember once taking a promotional tour with jazz pianist George Shearing, who traveled everywhere with his Guide Dog 'Lee.' We had boarded a flight early as allowed for

Norah Hamilton Straus is shown here with Labrador retriever puppies, one yellow and one black.
— **Photo from Guide Dogs for the Blind Archives**

those who need assistance. The pilot walked down the aisle of the cabin and struck up a conversation with George. Before we knew it, this nice man had offered to take 'Lee' outside for a walk before our flight. Well, just as he was bringing the dog back onto the plane, the other passengers began boarding. I'll never forget the stunned and confused looks on their faces. There was the pilot, the man who was going to fly the plane, with a Guide Dog! Surely a pilot couldn't be blind. They couldn't figure out what in the world was going on — and who could blame them?

In terms of the facility itself, the growth did not happen gradually. We were struggling along rather happily at the campus in San Rafael. I never envisioned anything like a building program that would create the kind of school we have today. Then one day Bill Johns showed me drawings of a new student building, saying 'Someday, this is what we are going to need.' Several years later, we embarked on an expansion program even more ambitious than the one he'd described. The project stretched over five hectic years, in which we replaced our outgrown plant with new facilities. During that time, we continued to raise puppies, train dogs and graduate 12 classes a year. Incredibly, we also completed construction of a new kennel complex, dormitory and separate administration building.

To me, the building program was a physical manifestation of how far we had come. It was like holding up a mirror to the success of the school and the efforts of everyone involved with it. When I looked at the new buildings, there was undeniable proof that Guide Dogs for the Blind had grown into a professional service organization. The little school that started in a rented house now occupied a beautiful, well-equipped campus. It was indeed a gratifying moment."

— *Norah Hamilton Straus*

6. The Move to San Rafael

The spring of 1946 brought important changes to Guide Dogs for the Blind. Construction was about to start at a new 11-acre site in San Rafael, where the breeding and training programs would be enlarged. After years of service, Lois Merrihew resigned to pursue her interest in horse breeding.

Named as her replacement was Capt. James Stanley Head, who was in charge of the Army K-9 Corps operations in the South Pacific during World War II.

The move to San Rafael was made possible by a building fund campaign organized the previous February, with what seemed like the ambitious goal of raising $150,000. The response from groups and individuals was better than anyone had dared hope. Within four months, $102,000 had been raised.

By the next spring, kennels large enough to house 100 dogs had been completed and plans had been drawn up for a dormitory with quarters for eight.

The expansion was needed. There were an estimated 13,000 blind people in California alone. Many of them were veterans who had been blinded in the war. From June, 1946 to June, 1947, 55 people applied to the school to receive Guide Dogs, but only 17 could be accommodated.

Among the applicants that first year in San Rafael were blind adults of various ages, occupations and educational backgrounds. As the school records show, "the blind person making application to this agency is very much the average; he is no different than the sighted person as to intelligence, education, background, desires and hopes for a normal life."

During that first year, 46 persons applied; 33 men and 13 women. Seventeen were between the ages of 18 and 25, 14 were 26 to 35 years old, seven were 36 to 45, five were 46 to 49 and three were 50 and older.

Education varied as well as age: 12 had attended grammar school only, eight had attended high school, 13 were high school graduates, five had attended college, three were college graduates and four were college students. The educational level of one student was unknown.

As for occupation, nine were factory workers, eight operated newsstands, six were students, four were housewives, three were machinists, two were musicians and two did not then have jobs. In addition, there was a judge, a leather worker, a rug maker, an upholsterer, a club executive, a piano tuner, a farm worker, a social worker, a vending machine operator, a salesman and a training officer for the blind. Thirteen of the applicants were also ex-servicemen.

Lois Merrihew left Guide Dogs to pursue her interest in horse breeding. She is shown here in 1989 with "Poncho," a quarter horse, on her ranch in Eureka, Calif.
—Photo by Thom Ainsworth, Guide Dogs For the Blind

This is the new complex made possible by the successful fundraising drive of 1946. The kennel buildings are on the right.
— *Photo from Guide Dogs for the Blind Archives*

Nine of these people had previously had dogs; 37 were to receive their first dogs.

Several profiles compiled that year by Guide Dogs staff provide a closer picture of students:

First, there is Sally, age 18, blinded since birth. A lovely, attractive girl, living with her mother and veteran brother. Sally has ability, a keen mind and deft fingers. She longs to be self-supporting and independent, but she was housebound. Her mother and brother work all day and so she had to sit at home alone. Now she has 'Lovely,' her new Guide Dog. 'Lovely' had opened a new life for Sally. She is taking training through the Vocational Rehabilitation Bureau and is learning a trade which will make her self-supporting. She can now go to church, sing in the choir, mix with young people of her own age—so it is no wonder that she is happier than she has ever been.

Then there is John, one of our young blind veterans, married to a wonderful girl. He resented having to ask her to lead him whenever he wanted to go forth. He requested a Guide Dog through the Veterans Administration and entered our school where he received 'Dolly.' At present he attends the University of Arizona and when he graduates he will not only have mastered the Liberal Arts, because he is very interested in such subjects, but he will have had a practical training in Poultry Raising. Already he is earning part of his way by breeding and racing pigeons. He claims his good fortune is all due to 'Dolly,' who has made these opportunities possible by giving freedom of motion.

Ralph was one of our more mature subjects, getting on to middle age. He lived alone in a small city, where he learned to do beautiful leather work. However, he could not sell it because he could not get around to buy his supplies or market his wares. He learned about Guide Dogs and thought one would give him the independence he desired. He was accepted into one of our classes and given 'Bertha.' Now he and 'Bertha' have become inseparable. The citizens of his town have become accustomed to seeing them striding down the streets at a good pace, going to the butcher, the baker and the leather supply stores. Ralph is developing his business rapidly, and what is more, he is spreading a wonderful feeling of happiness and contentment, all due to 'Bertha.'

Losing a dog guide after 10 years is a terrible experience. Mary discovered this when she had to put her faithful Seeing Eye dog to sleep. She did not want to take the long trip back to Morristown, N.J., for another dog—she could not afford the time or money. She was needed in her job,

where she does proofreading of Braille. Furthermore, she could not leave her elderly mother. She needed a new Guide desperately and fast. We made a place for her in one of our classes. She and 'Stella,' her new Guide, seemed to be made for each other the first time they met. Mary says she never knew there could be such a wonderful Guide Dog as 'Stella'—so may they have at least 10 happy years together.

The description ended on a note of respect for those who come to the school: "We could go on and on—because each student has a story—a story of courage, determination, ambition and accomplishment."

The building program was completed in 1948. The $61,500 main residence hall, designed by architect Vincent Buckley, housed four student rooms with two beds each, and quarters for trainer, housemother and cook. It also contained a fully equipped kitchen, dining room, lounge and office space for volunteer workers. A two-bedroom cottage for the supervisor of training was built at a cost of $9,000. Six new runs in the isolation kennel and five new runs for puppies between six and 12 weeks old were also built. A section of the gardens was planned and planted and an overall landscaping plan was approved.

In 1949, the school graduated its 100th student-guide team—Tony Barros of Trinidad, Colorado, and his dog "Butch." Other students in his class brought the total number of graduates to 110 by September, 1949, a remarkable record in little more than seven years.

7. Supplying Dogs, Selecting Breeds

Siberian husky, Dalmatian and German boxer are three of the breeds Guide Dogs tried before 1950 with limited success. Other breeds experimented with included flat-coated retriever, Chesapeake Bay retriever, Belgian sheepdog and Weimaraner, to name a few. This experimentation led to the three breeds now in use — German shepherd, Labrador retriever and golden retriever. About half of the dogs used as Guide Dogs today are Labrador retrievers with a quarter German shepherds and a quarter golden retrievers.
— Photo by George Wheeler

While Guide Dogs was moving from Los Gatos to San Rafael, it was making another important transition. It was changing from relying on donated dogs to establishing a breeding program.

German shepherds had been the preferred breed in the early days, partly because of their use by the Army K-9 Corps. Within a few years, other breeds had drawn attention.

In January, 1944, Guide Dogs began to get in touch with as many breeders, pounds and animal shelters as possible to secure dogs. It also set up booths at dog

shows to inform dog owners and breeders about the Guide Dogs program.

It soon became obvious that a breeding program would be necessary to meet the growing need for dogs. Guide Dogs set aside $1,000 in 1946 to buy breeding stock, deciding to use only stock of proven blood lines. Several local breeders donated stud service and excellent breeding stock.

The numbers show why a breeding program was crucial. In 1944, the school accepted 40 donated dogs; five, or 11 percent, were able to complete training. Of those, two were judged good enough for

An early student had a boxer as a Guide Dog and had this portrait taken. Graduates' dogs mean so much to them that it's not unusual for the graduates to have professional photographs taken and portraits drawn and painted of their prized canine friends.
—**Photo from Guide Dogs for the Blind Archives**

breeding although they were unregistered. In 1945, 29 dogs were donated, three completed training and six, including two males, entered the breeding stock. In the first half of 1946, 14 dogs were donated; two became guides. Between January, 1944 and July, 1946, Guide Dogs placed 26 dogs with blind graduates. Of those, 16, or 61 percent, were bred by Guide Dogs.

The ratio increasingly began to favor dogs bred by the school over donated dogs. Between July, 1946 and July 1947, 16 more Guide Dogs were produced; only six had been donated.

Careful treatment of the puppies from the moment of birth was increasingly emphasized.

The pregnant dog was put in a specially constructed wire pen five feet by 20 feet a week before the puppies were expected. The pups were born there and raised in the pen until they were eight weeks old.

Puppies received calcium and vitamins with every meal, their food was fed at body temperature and milk was part of the diet. Wire pens kept the pups clean and dry, reducing the danger of infections and parasites. Pens were portable and were rolled outdoors in sunny weather and indoors when it was windy or cold.

The school had a good idea of the best potential breeds and important characteristics of the dogs by 1948. It used mostly German shepherds, with a few Labrador retrievers, boxers and even one Norwegian elkhound. Two years later, new breeds had been added, including a Weimaraner, a Dalmatian and three Siberian huskies.

By 1965, the breeds used today had been selected — German shepherd, Labrador retriever and golden retriever. These breeds were chosen because of their availability, their adaptability to climate extremes and the fact that their coats are easy for a blind person to maintain.

Guide Dogs must be willing, dependable and completely fearless. Temperament and intelligence are primary factors. Size is also important; a dog must be able to fit onto a crowded bus and comfortably lie in cramped spaces near a blind person's work space.

Willingness, dependability, alertness and fearlessness shine in the face of this young German shepherd Guide Dog, photographed in the 1960s.
—Photo from Guide Dogs for the Blind Archives

8. Staff Growth

The staff grew as the school expanded and the number of students increased.

Guide Dogs had two licensed instructors and three apprentice instructors in 1949. A kennel manager and assistant, a cook and housemother completed the staff at the San Rafael campus. At the school's administrative office, still on Sutter Street in San Francisco, there were a social worker, membership secretary and office secretary.

William F. Johns, who would lead Guide Dogs from infancy to maturity during the next 20 years, was hired in 1949 as director. He replaced Earl F. Reinke, who served for two years after Capt. James Stanley Head.

As director, Johns shaped not only the program but the public perception of the school. Guide Dogs became known for its openness, warmth and humor as well as its excellent facilities and staff.

Dormitory Manager Lucille Price has supervised the kitchen since 1964. Of Johns, she commented, "I liked Mr. Johns very much, but then I wasn't alone. Everybody liked him. He was a big, good-natured man who always seemed to be laughing. You could hear him laugh from one end of the building to the next."

He was also, in the words of Norah Hamilton Straus, "a true genius with dogs as well as people."

Benny Larsen, his successor, described Johns as "very good at public relations and at representing Guide Dogs to the public, which was and still is a very important function. He came along at exactly the right time for the job that needed to be done."

The former assistant director of the K-9 Corps, Mr. Johns had known both Stewart Wiest and Clarence Pfaffenberger in the Army. During the war, he served with combat and service troops using dogs in North Africa and Europe. He developed the Army's post-war dog breeding program. Before the war, he had built a national reputation as a breeder of German shepherds and had taught at The Seeing Eye.

When he took over his new job, Mr. Johns made four major recommendations to the Board of Directors, all of which were approved and benefited the school over the long term.

He recommended that a general kennel manager be hired to administer the kennels and dog training and that a program for apprentice trainers be created. He also recommended that the breeding program be reviewed to improve the breeding stock, reduce the number of dogs rejected in training and provide more puppies and dogs of trainable age to meet the needs of the increased number of students. A production goal of 48 Guide Dog-student units was set for 1950, with progressive increases in future years.

He hired Carol Simonds, who ran the kennels from 1949 to 1959 and from 1964 to 1987. She was also a veteran of the K-9 Corps.

Mrs. Simonds had known Stewart Wiest, William Johns and Clarence Pfaffenberger in the Army. She had turned down an earlier offer from Guide Dogs to be a training instructor because she wanted to take care of dogs. Her chance came several years later when Mr. Johns offered her the kennel director's job.

"Were it not for Bill Johns and Eloise Heller—and later Norah Hamilton and Benny Larsen—Guide Dogs for the Blind would not exist. They were the spark, the

Under the direction of William F. Johns, Guide Dogs became known for its openness, warmth and humor as well as its excellent facilities.
—Photo from Guide Dogs for the Blind Archives

driving force," she said. "For me, taking care of dogs was what I wanted to do and I always felt very lucky to be able to work my whole life at what interested me."

Mrs. Simonds reported that even her arrival at Guide Dogs was lucky. She had planned to ask directions to the school when she got to San Rafael. "But, as I was standing at a street corner, I saw a Guide Dog instructor with a dark-haired woman led by a dog. I recognized the man right away as Stu Wiest, went over to him and he took me back to the school.

"The funny part is, the woman with him was Eloise Heller. Because she had a Guide Dog, I made the same mistake many people who first see a person with a dog in harness do—I assumed she was blind. It turned out Stu was giving her a demonstration on how the training works, so she could better explain the program in her role as president of the board."

Dormitory Manager Lucille Price with "Toby," a Shetland sheepdog presented to her by the Guide Dogs Board of Directors in 1989. Although he is not of a breed used by Guide Dogs, "Toby" daily accompanies Mrs. Price to work.
—Photo by Ed Smith

Mr. Johns hired Benny Larsen in 1958 as a kennel assistant. Mr. Larsen was a 35-year-old Danish dog trainer who had emigrated to Canada and then to the U.S. after World War II. He spoke little English at the time. Mr. Johns gave him a crash course in his adopted language.

"We were all expected to go into the community to make public presentations and Bill Johns put my name on the schedule like everybody else's," Mr. Larsen said.

"I was supposed to go into San Francisco, show a short film we had made about the school and then answer any questions. I objected, saying I could not speak well enough to do any such thing. But Bill Johns just smiled and told me it was my turn.

"So I did as I was told—and it turned out to be an awkward presentation, to no one's surprise. I had trouble operating the film and I stammered my way through the question and answer period. If it hadn't been for the help of one very nice lady, who helped with the projector, I probably would have destroyed the film. But I had to laugh about it and so did they.

"That was something I learned from Bill Johns—you can make a lot of small mistakes if you're willing to laugh at yourself, and people will respect you for trying. Not only that, you will learn more than you ever thought you could."

When Bill Johns died of cancer at the age of 56, the staff and students suffered a personal and a professional loss.

Bill Johns had accomplished what he had set out to do. He introduced his own exceptional German shepherd, "Frank of Ledge Acres," into the breeding program. The dog sired 162 puppies; 73 were used as Guide Dogs. Mr. Johns' comprehensive three-year program for apprentice dog trainers produced a high caliber of training staff personnel and maintained rigid training standards. He was instrumental in organizing volunteer area committees in California and the western states.

The school planted a fragrance garden at the entrance to the campus in his honor, inspired by the sprig of daphne he traditionally wore in his lapel each spring.

In Norah Hamilton, later Norah Hamilton Straus, Mr. Johns met his match for charm, intelligence and energy. For seven years — from 1962 when she was

Benny Larsen training a golden retriever to "stay." Mr. Larsen was hired in 1958 by William F. Johns as a kennel assistant and went on to become executive director, serving for 16 years in that position.

—Photo from Guide Dogs for the Blind Archives

"Frank of Ledge Acres", the result of a careful and highly selective breeding program himself, went on to sire 162 puppies; 73 became guides. Many of his descendants are now breeders and Guide Dogs. —Photo from Guide Dogs for the Blind Archives

elected to her first term as board president until Mr. Johns' death in 1969 — they joined forces to bring financial security and professional renown to Guide Dogs.

Her involvement with Guide Dogs was the natural cap on a lifetime of blind rehabilitation work.

Mrs. Hamilton was one of the well-known Powers models during her New York debutante days; she combined her modeling assignments with volunteer work at Bellevue Hospital.

As a volunteer firefighter in World War II, she acquired the skills to set up first-aid stations and devise evacuation plans for Boston hotels. She pioneered rehabilitation services for blind Navy men and developed programs to improve the morale of blind amputees.

After the war, she continued her volunteer work while traveling with her husband, Major General Pierpont Morgan

Hamilton, on military assignment. In Paris, she helped found Aid to French War Orphans.

A dog lover since childhood, she had also sought out Humane Societies wherever she had lived. When she and her husband retired in 1951, Guide Dogs offered a tailor-made outlet for her love of dogs and her commitment to the blind.

Mrs. Hamilton brought a vast store of talents to Guide Dogs. She knew the practical problems of the blind and how to harness the abilities of directorial boards. Her organizational energy was infectious. Her skill in creating successful fundraising events helped broaden the ranks of contributors and increased the public's awareness of the school during her 15 years as board president.

Guide Dogs for the Blind has always relied on private generosity for financial support. Operating expenses are met by large and small donations from civic groups, businesses, private organizations and individuals.

To ensure a steady flow of contributions, Norah Hamilton worked with Guide Dogs committees in many cities. One of the most successful events was the annual Pebble Beach Concours d'Elegance. The classic car show was sponsored by the Monterey County Committee of Guide Dogs, under the direction of Virginia Stanton.

The Concours and other annual events, such as a wine tasting sponsored by the Alameda County Committee, and the Women's Golf Assn. of Northern California tournaments held by the Monterey County Committee have not only raised money but introduced hundreds of people to Guide Dogs.

Norah Hamilton traveled the country on behalf of the school, making appearances on radio and television and before civic clubs. Several of these trips were made with jazz pianist George Shearing and his Guide Dog, a male golden retriever named "Lee."

"Between the three of us, it was hard to say who was the biggest scene stealer," Mrs. Hamilton joked. "I remember one radio show to which George had been invited primarily to play the piano. I was tagging along to put in a few words on behalf of Guide Dogs. Well, every time George paused in his playing, I started talking about the school. I had so much to say and so little air time to say it! I guess it would be fair to say I got carried away.

"Next time, Norah, I'd like a little less Hamilton and a little more Shearing."
— *George Shearing*

World-famous jazz pianist George Shearing and "Lee," his golden retriever Guide Dog. Norah Hamilton accompanied Mr. Shearing on many promotional tours as they spoke about Guide Dogs for the Blind.
—Photo from Guide Dogs for the Blind Archives

"The announcer was very nice and let me do it. So did George Shearing. The only thing he was more devoted to than 'Lee,' however, was his music. As we were leaving the radio station after the show, I turned to him nervously and asked how he thought it went. He gave me a good-natured smile and said 'Next time, Norah, I'd like a little less Hamilton and a little more Shearing.'"

Mrs. Hamilton also traveled abroad during her tenure, visiting similar schools in Europe. On those trips, her sense of humor sometimes proved even more of an asset than it was in the United States.

Norah Hamilton's involvement with Guide Dogs was the natural cap to a lifetime of blind rehabilitative work. She joined forces with Bill Johns to bring financial security and professional renown to the organization.
—Photo by Thom Ainsworth, Guide Dogs for the Blind

"Once, when we were staying at the Hassler Hotel in Rome, I had asked for the use of a movie projector," she recalled. "Not long afterward, I opened the door to find the assistant manager accusing me of showing pornographic movies! As it turned out, he had assumed that was what I was doing because a series of young men had been visiting my suite all afternoon. In those days, you see, only men were considered as candidates for guide dog instructors in Europe. That poor assistant manager was so embarrassed—to discover I had only been showing a film about our school to young men interested in becoming guide dog instructors."

With Bill Johns' death in 1969, a man of different background but equal leadership took the reins: Benny O. Larsen.

For Mr. Larsen, coming to Guide Dogs was a heroic achievement itself. He had joined the Danish underground in 1940, was drafted into the Danish Marines two years later and was taken captive in 1943 when the Germans defeated the Danish military. He spent four months in prison camp and then rejoined the underground.

After the war, he began training dogs in obedience and police work while he attended night classes at the University of Copenhagen. He became head of the police force for all of Denmark's military services. From 1948 until he emigrated to Canada with his wife, Else, in 1957, he spent his spare time training blind people to work with dog guides. The Danish practice was for instructors to visit students' homes for training.

"I had read a newspaper account of the school in San Rafael while I was still in Denmark. The program was much more sophisticated than what we had here at the time. I knew Guide Dogs would be a good place for me to work," he said.

The California State Board of Guide Dogs took an unusual action in 1958. It recognized Benny Larsen's expertise as an instructor by waiving its three-year apprenticeship requirement for him, making him a full-fledged Guide Dog instructor.

Mr. Larsen rose through the ranks at Guide Dogs, starting as a kennel assistant. There were only four instructors on staff in 1958, and one apprentice. The entire staff totaled 14.

"We worked on basically the same schedule the school has today—but we had only one instructor per class, instead of two. As they say, you had to love it."

Benny Larsen cites staff development as his single most important priority during his 16 years as executive director.

"My purpose and goal was for Guide Dogs to become the best-equipped school of its kind—speaking in terms of staff—that we could make it. One of the contributions I am proudest of is my decision to create the position of field representative. This is a staff person who travels to the homes of prospective students to interview them about everything that might affect their ability to have a dog—physical limitations, work and travel requirements, family concerns.

"The point is not to exclude people," Mr. Larsen said. "We want as many blind people as possible to have Guide Dogs. But it is best for all involved to be realistic from the start."

Mr. Larsen established the school's follow-up program. Every graduate still using a dog from Guide Dogs receives an annual visit from an instructor to answer any questions about the dog's care, behavior or guide work problems.

Satellite kennels where Guide Dogs can be taken for training problems or veterinary care were founded in Boring, Oregon, and Topanga Canyon in southern California under Mr. Larsen's direction.

The executive director's effort was to build what is now known as "quality control"—in everything from class instruction to meals served in the dining room.

To Benny Larsen, "the school actually operates as a unit, much like the blind person and the Guide Dog do. The cooperation and trust between the departments and everyone involved has to be there. There is a feeling of camaraderie that comes with working with the blind. We're all in the same boat so we make the best of it."

Benny Larsen, former executive director, is pictured in 1989 with a German shepherd Guide Dog. Mr. Larsen established the school's follow-up program.
—Photo by Jocelyn Knight

"I came to the school because I loved dogs and I was convinced they could do more than be watch dogs or police dogs or pets. I ended up getting so much satisfaction from watching blind people arrive barely able to go down the stairs and then—two weeks later—seeing them go out shopping with their dogs. It is a feeling I cannot adequately describe."
—Executive Director Benny O. Larsen

The gardens, buildings and grounds at Guide Dogs for the Blind are designed to merge practicality with beauty. The protected inner park allows students to enjoy the grounds during their free time with safety. Student dormitories are seen in the background.
—Photo by Thom Ainsworth, Guide Dogs for the Blind

"I came to the school because I loved dogs and I was convinced they could do more than be watch dogs or police dogs or pets. I ended up getting so much satisfaction from watching blind people arrive barely able to go down the stairs and then—two weeks later—seeing them go out shopping with their dogs. It is a feeling I cannot adequately describe."

Benny Larsen was succeeded in 1984 by former instructor and director of training Russell Post. A re-organization in 1989 created two new positions to replace that of executive director. Named the new chief executive officer was Bruce Benzler and chief operations officer was Thom Ainsworth. Following Guide Dogs tradition, both had come up through the ranks.

9. Rebuilding

Guide Dogs for the Blind embarked on a four-year, $5 million expansion plan to mark its 25th anniversary in 1967.

The master plan included the entire 11-acre campus, instead of only the five acres then in use. To allow the school to operate during construction, old structures were torn down only when the new replacements were completed.

The architects worked with landscape architects to design interiors and exteriors that complemented each other. Inside and out, practicality merged with beauty. For example, the entry drive not only allows smooth traffic circulation but also winds a graceful curve across the campus. The buildings are placed to create a protected inner park where blind people can walk safely. The fragrance garden named after Bill Johns is landscaped with plants marked in Braille.

The first of the three phases of construction was, not surprisingly, the kennels, which were relocated and expanded.

Three training kennels and separate kennels for receiving dogs and breeding and whelping the puppies were built along with the trainers' quarters, a puppy testing shelter and the kennel manager's residence. The kennel capacity enabled the school to triple the number of dogs while reducing maintenance costs because of new materials and labor-saving devices.

The second phase, construction of the student building, started in 1969. Classes had been filled to capacity for several years due to increased demand from blind men and women.

The new dormitory, which had eight two-bed rooms, was designed to make blind students comfortable as soon as they arrived.

Each room has its own dog run and separate floor-level sink for the dogs' drinking water. The rooms are close to the nurse's quarters, laundry, library, music and game rooms and the lecture room.

Outdoor graduation ceremonies are held on the patio that adjoins the dormitory. The patio leads to a park where students may relax after the day's training session. An outdoor swimming pool adjoins the dining room.

The final phase, the new administration building, was completed in 1971. The new building has offices for the chief executive officer and chief operations officer, student processing and social service, apprenticeship training, breeding selection, 4-H Club, puppy testing and evaluation, finance, membership and public information.

A west wing built onto the dormitory in 1981 added four more student rooms and the administration building was doubled in size in 1988.

III. Our Dogs

"I was raised on a farm outside Fresno in the San Joaquin Valley, where livestock animals are a large part of daily life. My sister and I became involved with the 4-H Club as soon as we turned nine, which is the youngest age allowed. We raised beef—mostly Hereford cattle—and hogs to show and auction at the county fair. At that time, Clarence Pfaffenberger was going to fairs and 4-H Club meetings looking for youngsters to raise Guide Dog puppies. As soon as I heard about the program, I applied as one of my club projects. When I was approved to raise a puppy, it was Clarence Pfaffenberger who brought him to our house and told us how to take care of him.

It was up to us as farm kids to get the puppies into town and expose them to different people and situations. So my sister and I were always hatching plans for trips into Fresno. I think sometimes we learned more than the puppy. We were lucky to have a gentleman named Gib Rambo—who is now the head of the S.P.C.A. in Fresno—lead obedience classes with our club. His association with our program also went all the way back to the K-9 Corps, where he knew Bill Johns.

I raised three puppies through 4-H and my sister raised four. Later, I worked for Gib Rambo's kennel after school, and had a chance to gain experience training private dogs. After I finished high school, Gib asked me if I'd ever considered entering the apprenticeship instructor program at Guide Dogs. The more I thought about it, the more I liked the idea. By then, I was in my first year of college and had gotten married. So I spoke to Bill Johns and he invited me to San Rafael for a tour and an interview. Not long after that, I received a letter saying I had been accepted and giving me a starting date.

My introduction to Guide Dogs was arriving at the school and being immediately blindfolded. From that moment on, there has been no looking back. I have been completely immersed in my work at the school.

I went through my blindfold training with a female German shepherd, sharing a dormitory room with a blind student for two weeks. I found him and other students to be helpful and sensitive to my situation. Being under blindfold was emotionally trying. I had moments of doubt and concern but I was continually encouraged to progress through the program and work the dog.

I look back now and compare the anxiety I had when I was under blindfold to the difficulty of blind people coming here for the first time. It made me realize how disorienting blindness is and how important it is, therefore, for us to make this school their temporary home. With each new class that arrives, the instructors must create a bond with their students so they become confident and comfortable

"What we do here has no secret formula. We have developed a system that works, which we repeat anew with each entering class. In doing so, we give the blind people who come here a life they wouldn't otherwise have. It's like that old joke about how to get to Carnegie Hall: practice, practice, practice."
— *Chief Executive Officer Bruce Benzler*

Chief Executive Officer Bruce Benzler exchanges greetings with a German shepherd on the Guide Dogs campus.
—Photo by Barbara Davis Treadwell

Now chief executive officer, Bruce Benzler is pictured here in August, 1957, as a 4-H member involved in puppy raising for Guide Dogs for the Blind. He is the third youngster from the left.
— Photo from Guide Dogs for the Blind Archives

here as individuals. Of course, it helps when the instructors keep a sense of humor — and that's one thing our instructors are known for. Because anything can happen in a Guide Dogs class.

Once, for example, we had two students rooming together, one of whom was an older man and the other was younger and also happened to wear dentures. Well, the older gentleman found the physical part of the training tiring. His calf muscles were getting sore, so he got some deep heating rub, which he kept on the top shelf of the medicine cabinet. The other student had a tube of denture adhesive, which he kept on the lower shelf. One day by mistake, they got their shelves mixed up. So one guy wound up with denture glue on his calves and the other guy had deep heat creme on his dentures. Fortunately, they were both able to see the funny side of the situation.

With each phase of my three-year apprenticeship, my commitment and enthusiasm grew. I remember the pride I felt when I passed the state board exam. You take an oral examination one day and the next day you're given a blindfold test. I took the test in early May; everything in the previous three years had been leading up to those two days. For every instructor, taking the state board exam is a big challenge. You have to be well-read on blindness and the various diseases that cause it as well as be familiar with all the state and federal agencies that provide services to the blind. Not to mention, of course, being able to work a dog on a demanding route selected by the examiners.

Like many new instructors, I originally came to the school out of an interest in training dogs. But after I'd had a chance to work with a class and see the students reach their goals, I realized that the real satisfaction comes from teaching and developing safe, effective units. For me, working with different types of dogs and then seeing them bond with members of the class into successful working teams is the ultimate sense of accomplishment.

The work we perform at Guide Dogs may seem mysterious to some. Many people have a hard time comprehending how it is possible to train dogs to lead blind people through today's world. The reality is, our program is methodical and predictable. In order to make it all work we need, first, a good sound product. In that regard, our breeding program is essential to having a good-quality dog. Then we need the 4-H Club involvement. We must have these youngsters and their families raise our puppies in their homes.

When the dogs return to us, we must have a professional staff that understands what needs to be accomplished within six months. We must bring out the best in each dog so it becomes a safe and effective guide.

Carrying that idea into class, it is crucial that the instructors make the best possible matches between dogs and students. Finally, in teaching the class, the instructors must ensure that those student-dog units leave here working well as teams.

What we do here has no secret formula. We have developed a system that works, which we repeat anew with each entering class. In doing so, we give the blind people who come here a life they wouldn't otherwise have. It's like that old joke about how to get to Carnegie Hall: practice, practice, practice."
— Chief Executive Officer Bruce Benzler

10. Puppy Testing

It's a warm morning on the San Rafael campus. Across a field of dense grass, a puppy takes his first walk on a leash. Today, he and other puppies from the school's kennel will be judged on agility and alertness, performing a series of tasks for testers with clipboards.

Every Thursday morning for more than 40 years, a devoted group of volunteers has assembled at Guide Dogs to participate in a tradition with equal parts purpose and appeal: puppy testing.

The puppy testers remove the puppies, one by one, from the kennel. Then, for two hours, they have the pleasure of watching them engage in some of the cutest behavior any dog lover has ever seen. Puppies climbing stairs. Puppies being weighed and measured. Puppies tumbling over their own paws as they chase after balls.

There is another aim behind all the play and affection. The sessions are designed to compile a record of a puppy's behavior.

"We start the puppies when they are about six weeks old and work with them once a week for five weeks," said MoZelle Zimmer, chief puppy tester since 1952.

"We don't teach the dogs; we observe them. Our job has two objectives. First, to take the puppies out of the kennels and love and pet them. Second, to build a file on the puppy's temperament and physical characteristics. It's very important to match the personality and size of the person with that of the dog. That's why we have so many tests and marks for the puppies."

Puppy testing was the brainchild of Clarence Pfaffenberger. Under Mrs. Zimmer's leadership, it has evolved into a well-organized but fun-filled drill.

There are half a dozen categories of puppy testers in Mrs. Zimmer's staff of 32.

The groomers clean and brush the puppies before the testing begins. The measurers chart the condition of the dogs' teeth, eyes, ears and coats as well as their weights and heights. Heelers judge the pups' reactions as they are walked on leashes. Are they, for example, "friendly, happy, quiet, timid (or) frightened" as they leave the kennel? How do they fare, on a scale from poor to perfect, in climbing the steps? When told to heel, are they "eager and willing," do they "heel nicely," or do they "resist," "refuse to move" or "complain vocally"?

Testers working outdoors note puppies' reactions to pedestrians, stairways, street grates and cars approaching from various directions. They also test for "intelligent" responses, such as "following objects readily," "showing curiosity about unfamiliar objects and people" and "adjusting to the tester and the environment."

This is only a small portion of what is to come in the next 18 months for Guide Dog puppies. The training is so demanding that half do not become Guide Dogs. Those who do, however, go on to long careers of service well worth the time and expense invested in each. The average working life of a Guide Dog is eight to 10 years. Every day of this working life can make a world of difference to a blind person.

MoZelle Zimmer, chief puppy tester since 1952, works with a devoted group of 32 volunteer puppy testers in weekly sessions. The sessions are designed to socialize the pups and to observe them and also to build a file on their individual temperament and physical characteristics. Puppy testing, used around the world by groups working with dogs, is the brainchild of Clarence Pfaffenberger, former director of Guide Dogs for the Blind.
—Photo by Thom Ainsworth, Guide Dogs for the Blind

Top Left

A volunteer groomer, Patty O'Shea, washes a yellow Labrador retriever puppy's paw as the puppy uses the towel as a chew toy.

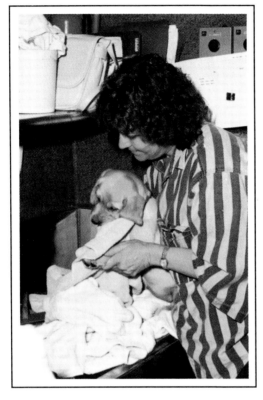

All photos on these two pages are by Thom Ainsworth, Guide Dog for the Blind.

Top Left

A volunteer groomer, Patty O'Shea, washes a yellow Labrador retriever puppy's paw as the puppy uses the towel as a chew toy.

Top Right

Another yellow Lab puppy gets measured. Growth is charted weekly.

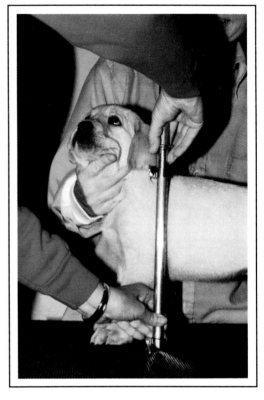

Bottom Right

It's important that a Guide Dog not be easily distracted, so puppies are tested on their reaction to their own images in a mirror. It's also important that the dogs are comfortable walking on any surface; that's the reason for the wire floor in the pen. Marge Zelles keeps a watchful eye on the pup.

Other testers take note of temperament. Does a puppy seem "at ease," "move about freely" and "assess a situation calmly"? They also take note of body sensitivity. Does the puppy "recover" and "retain composure" or "vocalize" in response to a gentle push? A final group of outside testers monitors puppies' reactions to the firing of a starter's pistol, rating ear sensitivity. Meanwhile, inside testers are busy evaluating "trainability," judging how quickly the puppies learn to sit, come and fetch a ball.

This is only a small portion of what is to come in the next 18 months for Guide Dog puppies. The training is so demanding that half do not become Guide Dogs. Those who do, however, go on to long careers of service well worth the time and expense invested in each. The average working life of a Guide Dog is eight to 10 years. Every day of this working life can make a world of difference to a blind person.

Top Left
A golden retriever pup tries the stairs with encouragement from the puppy tester.

Top Right
Pups are tested for ear sensitivity as volunteer Elizabeth Campbell fires a starter's pistol. Marge Zelles holds the leash.

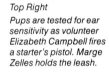

At Guide Dogs, the care that people must show these dogs so that the dogs will return it in lifelong devotion is evident all over the campus. There are dogs everywhere, from the Guide Dog the receptionist uses to the career-change dogs dropped from the program for any of a variety of reasons and adopted as pets by staff members. Others are breeding stock placed in the care of employees. Some are visiting for the day, brought by 4-H Club families or graduates on a trip to the school.

The dogs make themselves known audibly, too. A chorus of barks, blending the woofs of Guide Dogs in training with the yips of the puppies, arises periodically from the kennels.

Bottom Left
And successfully makes it to the bottom step as tester Elaine Mutrux looks on.

Top Left
Tester Nancy Peterson evaluates "trainability," seeing how quickly a puppy learns to fetch a ball.

All photos on these two pages are by Thom Ainsworth, Guide Dog for the Blind.

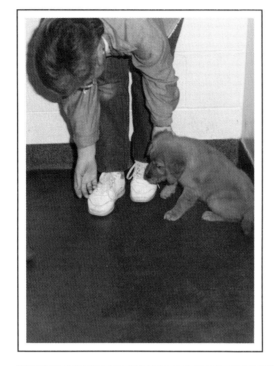

Top Right
Peggy ter Laare pays attention to a yellow Labrador retriever puppy.

Bottom
Three German shepherd pups enjoy the hugs of (from left) Elaine Mutrux, Ann Zolezzi and Betty Nelson.

Top Left
Ann Gregory cuddles a yellow Lab pup.

Top Right
Kids and puppies are a great combination. Here, Betty Nelson shows a yellow Lab to little girls. Hugs, cuddles, pats and compliments are part of the socialization of the puppies, every bit as important as the observation of their physical and mental makeup.

Bottom
A group picture of puppy testers taken in 1979 shows how much fun both testers and pups are having.

Top Left
Barbara Young pats "Kai."

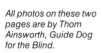

All photos on these two pages are by Thom Ainsworth, Guide Dog for the Blind.

Top Right
Jennifer Bassing interrupts her computer work to grab a rubber ball for (left) "Nordic," and "Puka."

Bottom
Betsy Irving gives double attention to (left) "Quiche" and "Willie."

Top Left
"Jubilee" guards her rawhide chew bone.

Top Right
"Samantha" contemplates life from the middle of the hall.

Bottom
"Flapper," (left) and "Bev" relax while Sue Sullivan works.

11. Kennels and Veterinary Care

The puppy testing that begins the dogs' training marks the end of another key part of the Guide Dogs program: breeding. The breeding program combines the best of "nature" and "nurture."

As for "nature," all Guide Dogs are bred, born and trained at the San Rafael campus. Clarence Pfaffenberger instituted the breeding program to augment the number of donated dogs in 1946. Geneticist Sherman Bielfelt has served as a consultant since Mr. Pfaffenberger brought him aboard.

Mr. Bielfelt keeps precise records, often dating back many generations, on each dog's blood lines.

As for "nurture," Guide Dogs creates the best possible environment for raising well-tempered animals, relying on puppy testing and placement in 4-H Club homes to avoid the personality problems found in kennel-reared dogs.

"I would say that the right selection of breeding stock contributes 30 to 40 percent to any particular dog becoming successful as a guide," said Paul Keasberry, director of puppy placement. "The better pups are pulled out to become breeders. If a litter is a combination of a dam and a sire already known to be excellent, those pups are tagged early and watched carefully."

Breeders are selected by a committee that meets every week to consider different dogs, comparing the genetic information provided by Mr. Bielfelt with the staff's own observations.

"In one year, we might pull 70 or 80 dogs as breeders," Mr. Keasberry stated. "That's our target number. Typically, we have to replace about 40 dogs a year among the breeding stock."

Over the years, the school has developed a system that provides the best possible care during breeding and whelping.

"We have about 165 breeding stock dogs, male and female, who live with families within a 50-mile radius of the school," Kennel Manager Dana Cunningham said.

"The females are brought into the whelping kennels for their three-week seasons; the males come in for three days when the females are especially fertile. Both go back home after mating.

"The females come back about two months later, before giving birth. They are brought in earlier to get settled in. They have everything they need to help them during birth. For example, Dr. Craig Dietrich, our veterinarian, can take x-rays or do a Caesarean section if necessary."

Puppies stay with their mother in the kennel for the first six weeks, three weeks in a whelping box where the mother is fed twice a day. When they are three weeks old, the pups are put on the floor with shredded paper and begin to explore and eat solid food. They are started on a "puppy mush," dry puppy food soaked in liquid, mixed with meat and fed from a specially designed pan. During this third week, they are offered food three times a day, but still rely on their mother for much of their nutrition.

At four weeks, puppies are separated from their mothers for brief periods; at five weeks, they are taken away all day and stay with their mothers overnight. The weaning process is complete when they are six weeks old. The mother dog returns home about one week later, after her milk has dried up.

Guide Dogs veterinarian Dr. Craig Dietrich checks over a German shepherd Guide Dog in training while instructor Cathie Laber and four clinic "office dogs" look on. They are (counter-clockwise) "Rolly," "Tunnel," "Rinny" and "Boo Boo."
—Photo by Thom Ainsworth, Guide Dogs for the Blind

The breeding and whelping kennels are off-limits to everyone except kennel and veterinary staff, but visitors can see the puppies and their mothers on a closed-circuit television monitor. Once the pups are weaned, they graduate to the puppy kennel, where they begin their exposure to the outside environment by contact with groups of volunteer puppy testers and puppy socializers. Between two and three months, the pups are placed with 4-H Club youngsters, who raise them as part of their families for about a year.

Each young dog must be in perfect physical condition before it leaves with its 4-H family. Between six and 10 weeks, the puppies receive worming treatments, shots and vaccinations. Any minor corrective surgeries, such as hernia and eyelid operations, are also performed then.

The other kennels are designed with as much thought to the dogs' needs as are the breeding and whelping kennels.

"All the kennels have radiant heat from the floors and the two that house the puppies also have forced air heat to keep their area warmer," the kennel manager said.

"Each kennel building has skylights as well as incandescent lighting. The interiors are stainless steel and there is water available at all times. All the kennels also have spacious runs with indoor/outdoor access. They are arranged so that, at any time of the day, the dogs can find some shade," Ms. Cunningham explained.

To keep track during puppy testing, litter-mates are first identified by a system of shaved spots on their fur. The system is designed to permit as many markings as there are pups: left shoulder, left hip, right shoulder, right hip. One puppy may be shaved only on the right shoulder, for example, while another is shaved on both the right shoulder and the left hip.

Between two and three months, the puppies are also tattooed inside their ears with an identifying mark composed of one letter and two numbers. This tattoo allows them to be identified throughout their lives if they get lost or are stolen.

Naming the puppies is treated with the same kind of care as their birth and early life.

Before the puppies go home with 4-H Clubbers to be raised, they are named by the puppy placement department. With so many pups, finding a name for each proves a challenging task.

A new pup cannot be given the name of any other dog currently working, whether it is a guide, a breeder, a dog in training or another puppy.

Names must be short, so that commands can be given concisely. Finally, a name must be found that strikes the right balance between dignified and unusual, but not so uncommon as to sound strange. "Duncan" might be used, but "Dannamead" probably would not.

When a dog dies or retires, its name may go back into circulation. Career-change dogs' names can be used again for breeders or active guides. Once a dog is named, that name follows it throughout its life.

Each new litter is assigned a letter alphabetically in naming the puppies. For example, a litter of German shepherds might be given the letter "T." Each puppy in that litter would be given a name beginning with "T." The next litter, regardless of breed, would be assigned the letter "U."

Here, for example, are the names of a litter of 10 German shepherds. The females were named "Trista," "Twix," "Therese," "Tangie" and "Tiffany." The males were named "Terence," "Taber," "Tate," "Telly" and "Tudor."

12. Training the Dogs

Potential Guide Dogs live with 4-H Club families from 10 weeks until about 15 months. The families love them, socialize them and teach them to obey basic commands.

When the young dogs are 14 to 16 months old, the 4-H families return them to the school to begin their formal training. The returning dogs receive physical examinations and are observed in isolation for two weeks before being transferred to the training kennels.

Guide Dogs must not do many things that most dogs do, for example, chase cats. This young German shepherd was trained not to give in to the impulse by the late Fred Maynard, director of the 4-H Department at Guide Dogs for the Blind, with the aid of a passing tabby.
—Photo from Guide Dogs for the Blind Archives

For five months, the young dogs are worked, fed and exercised by their instructors. Each instructor is assigned a string of 15 dogs, females and males from each of the three breeds.

"The best advice I was ever given was whatever you think you know about dogs, forget it. Every dog is an individual. You must be able to read it in order to give it instructions," said Thom Ainsworth, who trained dogs for the Air Force before coming to Guide Dogs in 1967. "The type of instructor we need is a rare find. Many people work well with dogs, but the true object here is the blind person's mobility. If you're thinking dog, not mobility, you won't hit the mark."

"The type of instructor we need is a rare find. Many people work well with dogs, but the true object here is the blind person's mobility. If you're thinking dog, not mobility, you won't hit the mark."
— Thom Ainsworth, Chief Operations Officer

Instructor Michele Pouliot
teaches ''Glider,'' a golden
retriever Guide Dog in
training, to avoid
obstacles.
—*Photo by Thom Ainsworth,*
Guide Dogs for the Blind

The program begins with basic obedience — mastering the commands "come," "sit," "fetch," "down" and "stay." Next comes the first guide work training — teaching the dog to work in harness. From the start, instructors train the dogs under real-life conditions, gradually introducing them to increasingly complex situations.

"After six or eight work-outs on a back road, the instructor is ready to take the dog to a quiet residential area of San Rafael, where it can concentrate without too many distractions," he said. "Then, slowly, they work into the more heavily trafficked areas."

The dogs learn the three fundamentals of guide work: left and right turns, street crossing and checking for curbs. It almost seems as if a Guide Dog can tell the difference between red and green traffic lights, but what's happening is that the handler is actually directing the dog to cross the street. The dog disobeys only if crossing is unsafe.

The dogs are also taught to maintain a straight line while walking in harness, a task accomplished by keeping the dogs moving steadily forward.

When a dog can perform those commands on a side street, it progresses to a busier area where it must contend with the overstimulation of a city — cars, pedestrians, strange noises and scents and unfamiliar objects.

"It's a matter of practice and conditioning. The first time a dog encounters an obstacle, it's going to bump you into it. So you have to scold it by making a bit of a commotion."

Guide Dogs must be comfortable in buildings as well as outdoors. Instructors such as Cathie Laber, shown here with a yellow Lab, take dogs through grocery stores, shopping malls, office buildings and restaurants as part of their training.
—Photo by Thom Ainsworth, Guide Dogs for the Blind

For example, a dog walking by a garbage can on a sidewalk may not move far enough to one side to allow the blind person enough room to pass. The trainer would react by banging the can, delivering a verbal reprimand and dropping the dog's harness. The dog and trainer would step back and try again. It is through reaction and repetition like this that the process of training occurs.

A command unique to guide work comes into play at this time: "hop-up." The command is used to focus the dog's attention in several situations, for example, when it dawdles or balks at an obstacle.

Once a dog responds well to commands and can concentrate on street routes despite distractions, it begins work indoors, where a whole new set of problems presents itself.

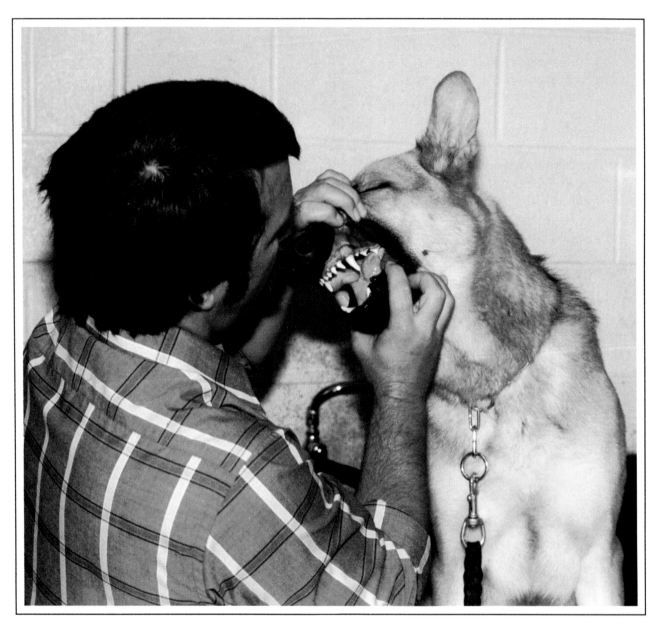

Trainers keep a constant eye on the health of the dogs, reporting any problems to veterinarian Craig Dietrich. Here, instructor Bob Wendler checks the teeth and gums of a German shepherd in training.
—*Photo by Thom Ainsworth, Guide Dogs for the Blind*

"A dog must be equally comfortable in a building as on a sidewalk," Mr. Ainsworth explained. "It must learn to walk on any surface and in spaces as narrow as store aisles. As a result, our instructors take dogs through shopping malls, office buildings, restaurants, into elevators and up and down different flights of stairs as a routine part of their training."

Guide Dogs for the Blind does not encourage the use of escalators by its students and dogs.

After 15 to 20 workouts, the dog and instructor must complete a "preliminary blindfold check." The dog leads the blindfolded instructor on a set route through downtown San Rafael. Each dog is graded, and if the performance is not satisfactory, the dog is sent back to an earlier stage of training or dropped as a potential guide.

Dogs who pass the check go on to another test that can be a shock to those who have never seen it: the preliminary traffic check. The goal is to give the dogs a healthy respect for moving vehicles.

"On a staged route that the dog and instructor have worked before, a car driven by a highly skilled member of our staff will turn in front of the dog to let it know it is supposed to stop," he explained. "Sometimes, the dog is bumped slightly by the car, to impress upon him not only the need to stop but also to back up to protect the blind person."

The test has been known to draw extreme reactions. One San Rafael housepainter became so irate at seeing a dog seemingly hit by a car that, in an effort to help, he fell off his ladder. Luckily, he landed unhurt in the bushes.

As the dog successfully stops and backs up during a traffic check, it is praised profusely. The instructor later includes encounters with cars of other descriptions so that the dog does not associate only one particular car with the "accident."

The training advances through increasingly challenging locations.

On busy Union Street in San Francisco, the dog must maneuver in crowds of fashionable shoppers and around sidewalk stands and outdoor cafes. At the San Francisco Civic Center, dogs learn to use revolving doors and ignore pigeons in a city park.

In Chinatown, they must deal with a crush of people and the stimulating smells from open-air markets. In Union Square, they must work as guides in elegant department stores. At Bay Area Rapid Transit stations and on the municipal buses, they master public transportation.

Instructor Annie Lerum takes a German shepherd for a preliminary blindfold check. Dogs who pass go on to another test that gets the attention of those who have never seen it before, preliminary traffic check.
—Photo by Thom Ainsworth, Guide Dogs for the Blind

Top

Most dogs wouldn't be able to resist chasing one pigeon, let alone dozens. Guide Dogs, of course, must be trained to ignore the temptation. Instructor Cathie Laber takes a yellow Labrador retriever through busy Union Square in San Francisco, known around the world for its pigeon population.
—Photo by Thom Ainsworth, Guide Dogs for the Blind

Bottom

"Foster," a golden retriever, gets a hug and praise from instructor Don Frisk after a workout in the plaza in front of City Hall in San Francisco in this photo, taken in 1986. "Foster," appropriately, now lives with a graduate in Golden, Colorado.
—Photo by Jim Gordon

Chinatown's crowds and tantalizing smells from restaurants and open-air markets might distract any other dog, but Guide Dogs are trained not to be distracted. Here, instructor Pete O'Reilly and a golden retriever Guide Dog in training walk through the tourist attraction.
—Photo by Thom Ainsworth, Guide Dogs for the Blind

"We scouted many areas and chose those that are ideal for what we need because they cover the range of environments a blind person is likely to encounter," Mr. Ainsworth said.

The dogs are put to the ultimate test a month before the class of blind students arrives. They must navigate the chaotic street scene along Telegraph Avenue in Berkeley near the University of California campus.

"There are all types of people and distractions on Telegraph Avenue, from street vendors to other dogs to musicians to difficult people," he remarked. "If a dog can handle that area of Berkeley, it can probably handle anywhere."

Watching the dogs work in hazardous places can be such an impressive experience that the Guide Dogs seem to take on heroic stature. Alert but calm, they avoid dangers their masters do not even perceive — scaffolding, awnings, parked cars, flagpoles, potholes and panhandlers. For the observer, the emotional impact can approach seeing someone rescued from impending disaster.

Watching the dogs work in hazardous places can be such an impressive experience that the Guide Dogs seem to take on heroic stature. Alert but calm, they avoid dangers their masters do not even perceive — scaffolding, awnings, parked cars, flagpoles, potholes and panhandlers. For the observer, the emotional impact can approach seeing someone rescued from impending disaster.

"The general public, which is not familiar with how a Guide Dog is trained, is astounded," said Chief Executive Officer Bruce Benzler.

"People think something magical is happening. But those of us in the business understand the hard work behind every successful dog. We know that every good Guide Dog results from three things: good breeding, good training and a good blind master."

Top

Hazardous situations, such as this one, in which a Guide Dog must walk in front of a construction truck, over an uneven plywood surface, and around a hose are part of the training. Here, a yellow Labrador retriever guides instructor Cathie Laber through the maze.
—**Photo by Thom Ainsworth, Guide Dogs for the Blind**

Bottom

Cable cars are a major attraction for visitors to San Francisco, but to a Guide Dog, they're just another traffic hazard. Here, instructor Pete O'Reilly trains a yellow Lab.
—**Photo by Thom Ainsworth, Guide Dogs for the Blind**

Top
After a hard morning's training workout, Guide Dogs in training have a 45-minute "recess," also called a community run. Instructors are, left to right, Terry Barrett, Cathie Laber and Dave Byerley.
—Photo by Thom Ainsworth, Guide Dogs for the Blind

Bottom
Kim Jacobson takes the rigorous state examination that will qualify her as a licensed instructor. The test is conducted on an unannounced route in Sacramento. With her is "Macho."
—Photo by Thom Ainsworth, Guide Dogs for the Blind

IV. The 4-H Program

"I first became involved with the puppy raising program when I was 12 and lived in a tiny town called Ophir outside Auburn, California. I decided to raise a Guide Dog puppy through the 4-H program for two reasons. First, I had an uncle who had lost his sight from glaucoma, so I had a special interest in the problems of the blind. Second, I'd always loved animals. Looking back, it was pretty simple: I wanted a puppy and I wanted to do something to help somebody else.

My parents had a cattle and fruit farm so I was accustomed to raising animals and then learning to part with them. Even so, the first time I raised a Guide Dog puppy, it was a heartbreaker to give him up. He was a German shepherd named 'Caleb' and I was still pretty young. I remember the man who received 'Caleb' was from Texas. He was in a band there and, when I met him at graduation day at Guide Dogs, it was obvious he dearly loved the dog. He even promised to give him ice-cream cones like I had.

I never saw 'Caleb' or the man from Beaumont again, but raising the puppy and meeting his blind owner made me feel good about myself. I knew that my dog was going to help someone and that took away a lot of the sadness.

Not long after 'Caleb' left, my mother and I were in Auburn and happened to walk by the county courthouse and see a blind man with a dog. That night, I went home and filled out my second application for a Guide Dog puppy. So within a short time we had another one, a German shepherd named 'Flare.'

We raised her and she became a brood bitch living at our home, which made the whole family very proud. Later, she was retired and we kept her as our family pet until she died.

After 'Flare,' we raised three more German shepherds for Guide Dogs before I went away to college. Then I got married and we eventually moved to a small country town named Wallace, in the Sierra foothills.

One source of real satisfaction for me has been the involvement of our daughter, Deborah, in puppy raising in the last few years. It was the first project she wanted to participate in when she joined 4-H. She started when she was 10 and is now on her fifth dog. We've had three German shepherds and are currently raising our second yellow Labrador retriever.

When Debbie applied for her first puppy, a 4-H leader came to interview us at our home. At that time, we discussed how I had also done this as a child. Now it's become a family project again. Debbie is really the trainer, though I'm like the grandmother who can spoil the kids and get away with it. We're proud of our daughter for being so good with the puppies. She takes them to all the 4-H field days she can and often comes home with an award for obedience. She's already a junior leader in 4-H and hopes to become a veterinarian.

"Even after Debbie grows up and goes to college, I expect us to keep raising puppies as a retired couple. I imagine that Debbie will someday continue the program with her own children. The dogs are really a vital part of our existence. I don't know how we would act without them."
— Linda Chaddock

Tracy Farlow of San Jose, Calif., one of Guide Dogs' 4-H Club puppy raisers, shows the love and affection the club members pour into raising each dog, only to give it up at the end of a year or so. The greatest reward for the puppy raiser comes when the dog she or he has brought up becomes a Guide Dog.
— Photo by Thom Ainsworth, Guide Dogs for the Blind

We take the dogs everywhere we can. They go to school; they go to sports events; they go shopping in town. The principal and everyone else at Debbie's school are behind the project. The high school district secretary is a 4-H leader. So the kids take the dogs into the classroom. Debbie even takes them into the gym for sports practice.

Our particular 4-H Club group also plans an outing once a month. We arrange to go to a function together, like an agriculture show, the Asparagus Festival or the airport. We'll take a bus so the dogs can gain as much exposure as possible. There isn't a day that the puppy we are raising doesn't go somewhere with a member of our family.

If we have any problems, we call Guide Dogs for the Blind and talk to Geri Owens or someone else on the puppy placement staff. Geri has just been great. She answers any questions Debbie has about the dogs, and she comes to most of the 4-H field days.

Even after Debbie grows up and goes to college, I expect us to keep raising puppies as a retired couple. I imagine that Debbie will someday continue the program with her own children. The dogs are really a vital part of our existence. I don't know how we would act without them. They're fun, they teach responsibility and they help us meet people. But knowing that a dog we raise helps someone who is blind is the most rewarding part."

— Linda Chaddock

Puppy raiser Katherine Gordon of Rancho Palos Verdes, Calif., and "Folger" in 1987. "Folger" is serving as a Guide Dog in Anchorage, Alaska.
—Photo by Jim Gordon

13. Raising a Puppy

Soon after the breeding program started, Clarence Pfaffenberger knew he had to find a way to raise the puppies in loving homes. Fortunately, he struck upon the idea of linking the Guide Dogs program with the 4-H Club.

Ever since, the club has provided an ideal method of rearing and socializing the puppies. Raising a Guide Dog is a nationally accredited 4-H project. 4-H members in the eight Western states of California, Oregon, Nevada, Washington, Arizona, Utah, Idaho and Colorado provide well-socialized young dogs for the school.

Paul Keasberry, director of puppy placement, serves as department head of the 4-H program.

"The overall purpose of our puppy placement program is two-fold," he explained.

"The first objective is to teach the puppy what we call 'house manners'— to behave properly indoors. This includes such things as basic obedience, housebreaking, staying clean, not eating off tables and counters, not jumping up or growling at visitors.

"The other purpose is what we call 'socialization.' Basically, it refers to the process of exposing the puppy to as many different situations and environments as possible and in a positive manner. We want the puppy at an early age to develop the confidence to go anywhere at any time with anybody—whether it's for a walk in the park or a ride on public transportation.

4-H puppy raisers are encouraged to expose the young dogs to public transportation. Here, a 4-H Club member leads a young yellow Lab off a bus.
—*Photo by Thom Ainsworth, Guide Dogs for the Blind*

For those 4-H Club members whose puppies go on to become guides, the high point comes on graduation day. In a final touching moment, the 4-H'ers walk forward, one by one, on stage with the dogs and present them to the blind graduates.

"Puppies need to grow up in a warm, loving, family atmosphere rather than in a kennel situation. Being raised in a family makes the dogs able to relate to and work for human beings instead of having their main focus be other canines."

About 725 youngsters are participating in the program at any given time. About a thousand families regularly raise puppies. The school relies on local 4-H leaders in counties throughout the West to coordinate such a large effort. These leaders interview prospective families and act as liaisons with Guide Dogs. School policy also sets certain standards.

"We ask that the whole family be supportive of the project," Mr. Keasberry said. "We require that the yard have some sort of fenced area where the puppy can be kept when all members of the family are occupied. And we ask that the puppy live in the house and be socialized as a member of the family."

Most of the puppies are raised in rural areas, but any location meeting the requirements is welcome.

During puppy raising, Guide Dogs staff members are available to give 4-H Club members as much professional care and expert advice as they need. Each puppy raiser receives a Guide Dog collar, leash and a small supply of food. A raiser's manual describes in detail how to take care of the puppy.

Before your puppy arrives:
- Prepare a bed or a sleeping box for your puppy.
- Obtain a lightweight chain with at least one swivel on it.
- Choose a food and water dish.
- Make your yard fence dog-tight. You may want to build a run for your puppy.
- Select a comb and a stiff brush for daily grooming of your puppy.

After your puppy arrives:
- Give your puppy time to relieve himself before he enters the house. Take him to the place where you will want him to go immediately.
- Give your puppy food and water; let him rest.
- REMEMBER: Your puppy needs affection, rest and time to explore and adjust to his new home. Training lessons can wait for a few days.

The manual provides instructions on building wooden beds and outdoor runs, the proper way to feed and care for the puppy, specific advice on recognizing and treating common ailments, obedience training, housebreaking, correcting and praising and suggestions on "the making of a Guide Dog."

For your puppy to be a successful Guide Dog you must:
1. **Rear him.** Teach him early in life what he can and cannot do to be well-behaved.
2. **Socialize him** to the world he will live and work in.
3. **Protect** his well-being to assure that he will grow to be a sound working dog.
4. **Train him.** Give him the joys of having a job to do and receiving praise for a job well-done.

After a year with the 4-H Club families, the puppies return as young dogs to the school to begin their training. The moment of truth arrives for each dog during that training: Will it become a Guide Dog?

"For a 4-H'er, there is nothing more gratifying than seeing a puppy he or she raised go on to become a Guide Dog," Mr. Keasberry said. "These youngsters and their families are truly proud of their dogs, as well they should be. And we at Guide Dogs are equally proud of our 4-H families."

The bond that develops between 4-H Club members and puppies is so close that young dogs who do not become guides often return as pets to the families that raised them. The rest have no trouble finding a new home. The excellent reputation of Guide Dogs has created a two-year waiting list for the adoption of career-change dogs.

For those 4-H members whose puppies go on to become guides, the high point comes on graduation day. In a final touching moment, the 4-H'ers walk forward, one by one, on stage with the dogs and present them to the blind graduates.

Puppy raisers often bring their pups to 4-H "Fun Days" held at the Guide Dogs campus. Here, a veterinarian checks the teeth of a young dog while the raiser looks on.
—**Photo by Thom Ainsworth, Guide Dogs for the Blind**

4-H Club members and dogs take a quiet break at a "Fun Day" on campus.
—**Photo by Thom Ainsworth, Guide Dogs for the Blind**

Thom Ainsworth found this note crumpled up and slipped behind the collar while doing a physical exam of a young dog returned from a 4-H family.

"Hey, that means me!" "Wizard," a yellow Lab pup, leans out the back of Orange County, Calif. 4-H Leader Pat Hoyt's station wagon.
—Photo by Thom Ainsworth, Guide Dogs for the Blind

Pups must have their water, and a 4-H Club member sees to it that this young golden retriever gets his.
—Photo by Thom Ainsworth, Guide Dogs for the Blind

V. *Our Graduates*

"I am the managing director of the Blind and Visually Impaired Center of Monterey County, which provides orientation-and-mobility and living skills training and services. I am 36 and have been blind since I was 22, when I lost my sight from complications of diabetes.

Because I went blind as an adult, I have the memory of sight. For instance, I recall colors. I grew up in Pacific Grove, where I still live, so I'm familiar with the surroundings. I remember the same cracks in the sidewalk that were there when I was a child.

One of the things I still miss terribly is the ability to just jump in my car and go for a drive. When I was first blind, that kind of freedom was totally gone. But now, thankfully, I have gotten some of that feeling back, because of Guide Dogs. I still can't hop in the car and drive off, but I can pick up my dog's harness and go out for a spontaneous walk, especially on a route I know.

I am now working with my second dog, a black Labrador retriever named 'Bobbi.' But it was getting my first Guide Dog that really changed my life. She was a golden retriever named 'Brama.' I was still quite ill at the time; I was on kidney dialysis. For the first three years of being blind, I was simply trying to stay alive. Then I began to work on my emotional adjustment. When I went to Guide Dogs the first time and got 'Brama,' I felt as if somebody had taken off my blindfold. I could walk down the street by myself for the first time in years. I was so excited. I remember running out of bread not long after I got home. So I went to the store with 'Brama' to buy some more. That single act made me so proud.

I think everyone grows from experience and losing my sight did of course change me. Then getting a dog changed me again. It made me more independent. I've always loved life and I certainly love my dogs. They contribute every day in some way to my happiness.

I've also benefitted in other regards from my relationship with Guide Dogs for the Blind. Going there for instruction was an uplifting experience. The staff is so friendly and caring. The campus is so beautiful—the gardens, the music room, the outdoor pool. The other students I met there were special people in the blind community. I learned a great deal from them, not only about how to use a dog but also psychologically. I've stayed close friends with a number of other graduates. Another great advantage to me is the follow-up the school provides. To be able to pick up the phone and call for advice if I'm having a problem is a real comfort.

They don't forget about you at Guide Dogs."

— *Kathy Wise*

At the 1989 wedding of Kathy Wise and Randy Henson in Monterey there were two special guests, the bride's Guide Dog, "Bobbi," decked out in a blue bow, and her retired Guide, "Brama."
—Photo by Donald E. Rossi

"I think everyone grows from experience and losing my sight did of course change me. Then getting a dog changed me again. It made me more independent. I've always loved life and I certainly love my dogs. They contribute every day in some way to my happiness."
— *Kathy Wise*

14. Selection of Students

Guide Dogs is the only such school in the United States to interview all applicants before they are accepted into the program.

Field Representative Vivian Carson, an orientation and mobility specialist, heads the school's program of advance interviews and follow-up visits. She spends much of her time traveling to the homes of those who want Guide Dogs.

"The reason we insist on the home interview is that people are quite different in person than they appear on paper," Ms. Carson said. "The interview tells us about their home environment, their ability to get around, the family's acceptance of a dog, the student's need for a dog and their physical ability to walk with a dog."

Guide Dogs is supported entirely by private donations; it makes no charge for the dogs or the instruction.

People who apply to become students are a select group; only about five percent of the blind population in the United States and Canada relies on canines instead of canes. Many blind people, like many sighted ones, simply do not like dogs well enough to own one. Others are not physically capable of caring for or working with a dog.

Still, the number of people who apply to Guide Dogs exceeds the number of openings. Typically, there is a waiting list of eight to 12 months. About half of the applicants are accepted after the first interview. Another 15 percent qualify eventually by improving mobility skills or making changes in living situations. The goal of the application process is to let people in, not exclude them.

"We're looking for a number of factors," she stated. "Is this person ready to look after a dog? What are the spouse's and children's feelings about having one? Does the person already have good mobility with a cane? Is this someone who is emotionally stable and in control?

"Basically, we want responsible people who are already traveling safely and independently in their home areas. That's because we consider using a dog as advanced mobility training, compared to basic training with a cane.

"I write a report after each interview to give the Guide Dogs staff all the information they need. The reports are used first by the eligibility committee to determine acceptance for training. Then they are reviewed by class instructors, so they have as much background as possible on the students. Do they live in a country area with no sidewalks, for example? Do they ride on public transportation?

"The other thing I'm doing in the interview is talking to applicants about our program. We want to make them feel as comfortable as possible when they arrive. So we try to give them a good idea of what their days here will be like.

"We tell them what to bring in terms of clothes and supplies. But we also let them know, for instance, that they will be getting a good deal of physical activity. After all, they will be working six days a week, walking routes with their dogs. Some people need to get in better shape first. When I'm out there, I do my best to give people a realistic picture. Often, I'll take a harness handle and pull it while an applicant holds on so he or she understands the pace of the dog."

Handling the communication with the applicants as well as travel arrangements and personal needs of class members is the responsibility of the Social Service Department.

"We do all the paperwork involved in processing the applicants and we offer basic personal services during class," said Sue Sullivan, director of social service. She has seen the classes double since she joined Guide Dogs in 1965.

"As the number of students has increased, the duties of our department have also grown," she remarked. "We

help students write letters and cards to their friends and families. We arrange for laundry and dry cleaning services if requested. We read mail to students.

"During the first two weeks of class, we also offer a shopping service. If students need something at the store, we will pick up those items on a designated day. For the last two weeks of class, of course, they are on their own in terms of shopping, because they can use their dogs to go to nearby stores."

Guide Dogs is the only school of its kind to provide annual follow-up visits to every graduate as long as he or she is still using a dog as a guide.

This allows instructors to catch any problems while they are in the beginning stages, instead of allowing early mistakes

to develop into bad habits. The visits make sure that the dogs are well cared for and give graduates an opportunity to ask questions.

"After students graduate, we keep track of all their correspondence," Sue Sullivan commented. "Twice a year, we mail out questionnaires on the dogs' physical well-being and how the guide work is going. If they have any problems, they are to let us know.

"We also handle the mailing of a tape-recorded version of 'Guide Dog News' four times a year, and, at Christmas, we send a taped Christmas greeting to our graduates. Finally, we work with the training department in notifying graduates when a representative will be there for an annual visit, and we help with travel arrangements for staff trips."

Top Left

Guide Dogs for the Blind is the only school of its kind to make yearly follow-up visits to all of its graduates using a Guide Dog. Here, instructor Kelly Martin visits graduate Barbara Browning of Petaluma, Calif., and her Guide, "Liddy," a yellow Labrador retriever.
—Photo by Thom Ainsworth, Guide Dogs for the Blind

Top Right

One of the major purposes of the follow-up visit is to be sure that the guide work is going well. Kelly Martin, Barbara Browning and "Liddy" take a stroll as Mr. Martin looks on, offering suggestions for improvement.
—Photo by Thom Ainsworth, Guide Dogs for the Blind

15. Coming Together for Class

Each new class of blind people at Guide Dogs is certain to contain members of both sexes, several races, different economic groups and many occupations.

The intensive training is an experience the class members will never forget. Life-long friendships, both human and canine, are made here.

For the school, each new class marks the end of two years of careful preparation. The kennel workers, veterinary and social services staff, trainers, harness makers, volunteers and 4-H Club families have all done their parts. Now the full-grown dogs who represent their joint efforts will take the final step into a lifetime of service.

The dogs go through final training checks, final traffic checks, and obedience tests as well as full physicals 10 days before the class begins. Just over half of the original string will have made the final cut.

For the students, the first few days of instruction are often marked by the tension of making a major life transition. They discover exactly what a dog can and cannot do, and, therefore, what they must and must not do. They begin to understand that there is no magical formula, only good training, hard work and mutual trust.

The students listen to lectures by their instructors on the care and feeding of the dogs during the first two and a half days of class. They are also instructed on how to use the harness. They are working only with an imaginary dog named

"Matching the right dog to the right person to create a unit that can work safely on the street is what Guide Dogs is all about. There is no way to overstate the importance of making a good match."
— *Chief Executive Officer Bruce Benzler*

A day's schedule for a Guide Dog student:

6:30 a.m.   — wake up
7:00 a.m.   — leash-relieve the dog
7:15 a.m.   — breakfast
8:00 a.m   — obedience exercise
9:00 a.m.   — load the bus for morning workout
11:45 a.m. — leash-relieve the dog
12:15 p.m. — lunch
1:15 p.m.   — load the bus for afternoon workout
4:00 p.m.   — back to campus
4:20 p.m.   — feed and leash-relieve the dog
5:00 p.m.   — lectures
6:15 p.m.   — dinner
9:00 p.m.   — night route workout during last week of training
10:00 p.m. — lights out
Students and dogs work six days a week for 28 days.

Students get their first experience using a harness during "Juno" workouts. "Juno" is the name for an imaginary dog whose role is played by the instructor. Here, instructor Bob Wendler holds one end of the harness while student James Riley of Sacramento Calif. holds the handle. This is the way the student learns how a dog will function in harness.
—Photo by Thom Ainsworth, Guide Dogs for the Blind

"Juno," really an instructor playing the part of a Guide Dog, to teach the students the commands and movements they will need to know.

The instructors are observing the students during this training, seeing how their physiques and temperaments match with the available dogs. A 100-pound person is not given an 80-pound dog; a quiet student is likely to receive an easygoing guide. Students' preferences in breed and gender are accommodated if possible.

"Matching the right dog to the right person to create a unit that can work safely on the street is what Guide Dogs is all about," said Bruce Benzler, chief executive officer. "There is no way to overstate the importance of making a good match."

In those first two-and-a-half days, the instructors gather all the available in-

Following the "Juno" workouts, student James Riley works with the real thing, his new yellow Labrador retriever "Nibben," while instructor Bob Wendler stays close. "Nibben" is keeping track of the position of the car at left.
—Photo by Thom Ainsworth, Guide Dogs for the Blind

The only reward a Guide Dog ever asks for its work and loyalty is praise and love. Student Dawn Bevans of Eugene, Oregon, distributes plenty of both after her very first workout with her new golden retriever Guide Dog, "Abby." **—Photo by Thom Ainsworth, Guide Dogs for the Blind**

formation to pair the dogs and students. They already know the temperaments, physical characteristics and abilities of every dog in their string because they have just spent five months training them. They develop a picture of each student, based on information from the home interview and their own observations from the "Juno" training.

The two instructors for the class and the class supervisor meet on the evening before the students receive their dogs and pool their information. Over several hours, they fit the individual pieces together into a single picture. One by one, they match dogs and students.

After a final morning of "Juno" training, the students receive their dogs. This first meeting marks the beginning of a bond rivaling that between any two human beings. In the following weeks, the dogs slowly transfer their loyalties from

Guide Dogs are trained to rest at their masters' feet during mealtime. Here, in a photo taken in the 1970s, a yellow Lab Guide Dog shows the true meaning of relaxation.
—Photo by Thom Ainsworth, Guide Dogs for the Blind

their trainers to their new masters as, together, they work the same locations the dogs first conquered during their training.

"What happens in class is the same sequence, in terms of instruction and exercises, as that of the dog training," Bruce Benzler said. "We start small, on a quiet back road. Then we progress to a residential street, downtown San Rafael, to San Francisco and Berkeley. The obstacles and commands are all the same, only this time we are teaching the student to work with the dog."

Gradually, a new entity emerges, a working unit of blind person and dog.

"Creating that unit is our real accomplishment," said Thom Ainsworth. "It's not training the dogs alone, or instructing the blind people in how to use them. It's putting both pieces together in a whole."

Psychologist Marla Merriam and her black Labrador retriever Guide Dog "Hyla" at the grand piano. A painting of her former Guide Dog "Bon Bon" is on the wall.
—Photo by Thom Ainsworth, Guide Dogs for the Blind

"You also have to allow for the dog in your relationships with others, much as you would a child. I dated one man, for instance, that 'Hyla' did not like at all. My present boyfriend, however, is so sweet with her. They've become fast friends. He talks to her as much as I do."
—Marla Merriam

"I am a 35-year-old psychologist with a practice in San Rafael now using my second Guide Dog, a black lab named 'Hyla.'

For me, one of the interesting aspects of having a Guide Dog is how it has changed me emotionally.

When I got my first dog—a yellow Lab named 'Bon Bon' that I had for 13 years as a guide and pet—I found a new freedom. More independence was the first thing I noticed. But I also recognized the emotional alliance with another being. For instance, before I got a dog, I used to be very paranoid about getting lost. I thought I was deficient in that area. With a cane, you only have yourself. There's no relationship. 'Bon Bon' really helped overcome that paranoia. For one thing, she was there. For another, she was a really good traveler. I could show her a route once and she would never forget it.

So what happened, in the natural course of things, was that I began to trust her judgment. Because, when it came to traveling, I knew her judgment was better than mine. As a result, I began to develop a better sense of control. No longer was I in the position of suddenly finding myself angry and frightened over being lost. 'Bon Bon' knew where we were, and I knew I could count on her to find our way.

But it was not just the sense of having more control to go and do things on my own. I also had to learn to say when I had needs. It's very important when you're disabled to ask for help in a balanced way. Typically, you are told by your parents either that you need help with everything or that you're just like everyone else and don't need special assistance at all. Too often, disabled people grow up with one extreme or another.

With 'Hyla,' I've had to learn to be very specific about my needs. She is different from 'Bon Bon' in that she doesn't memorize a route as quickly. So sometimes, when I am traveling to a particular place for the first or second time, I ask someone to meet me at the bus stop. This is something I have had to teach myself to express—when I need a small amount of help at the beginning, until 'Hyla' and I know where we are going. For me, this has been a process of growth and maturity.

Beyond that, of course, the relationship with the dog is always there for you. You have to learn to be giving in return. The dog is not a machine. It needs to feel included and rewarded. Having a Guide Dog is a 24-hour-a-day responsibility. If the dog is sick, you have to take care of it. If it's raining, you still have to take it out for a walk. You also have to allow for the dog in your relationship with others, much as you would a child. I dated one man, for instance, that 'Hyla' did not like at all. My present boyfriend, however, is so sweet with her. They've become fast friends. He talks to her as much as I do.

All of these changes, I suppose, can be summarized with one word: trust."
—Marla Merriam

Epilogue: Looking Ahead

For those who work at Guide Dogs for the Blind, Inc., the challenge lies not so much in breaking new ground as it does in maintaining a standard of excellence.

The program that has been built since the early 1940s demands constant vigilance. Each dog, each student, each working unit embodies the knowledge and experience of six thousand before it. Each instructor carries on a tradition of service first set by such extraordinary pioneers as Lois Merrihew, Bill Johns, Norah Hamilton Straus and Benny Larsen. The entire school honors the tradition.

Development Director Jennifer Bassing, whose department is responsible for the production of "Guide Dog News," for attracting donations and for corresponding with contributors, said of the school:

"If I had to say anything about the work we do, not only in the development department but also at Guide Dogs in general, it would be that we try to bring a sense of belonging to everyone who becomes involved here. We are that rare thing in today's world: a true community."

There may be new developments in the future. Thom Ainsworth predicts a time in the coming century when, through the use of new technology, Guide Dogs will be able to train students who are both deaf and blind.

Guide Dogs will always rest on a foundation of a single idea. That idea was expressed recently by Donald E. Rossi, past president of the Board of Directors, who quoted a man who was neither blind nor involved with dogs — but who understood what it meant to meet life's challenges: World War II aviation hero James Doolittle. Aptly, he was the first to fly "blind," relying entirely on cockpit instruments.

"Jimmy Doolittle said something that sums up not only why I became involved with Guide Dogs but why all the others have as well," Rossi said. These were Doolittle's words:

"I have a very simple philosophy of life. I believe we were put on this earth for a purpose. That purpose is to make it, within our capabilities, a better place in which to live. We can do that by painting a picture, writing a poem, building a bridge, protecting the environment, combating prejudice and ignorance, providing help to those in need or in thousands of other ways.

"Just so we serve."

Index

Index of Dogs' Names